Wonders

Reading/Writing Companion

Mc
Graw
Hill

mheducation.com/prek-12

Send all inquiries to:
McGraw Hill
1325 Avenue of the Americas
New York, NY 10019

ISBN: 978-1-26-577518-6
MHID: 1-26-577518-4

Printed in the United States of America.

3 4 5 6 7 8 9 LMN 26 25 24 23 22

A

Welcome to WONDERS!

We're here to help you set goals to build on the amazing things you already know. We'll also help you reflect on everything you'll learn.

Let's start by taking a look at the incredible things you'll do this year.

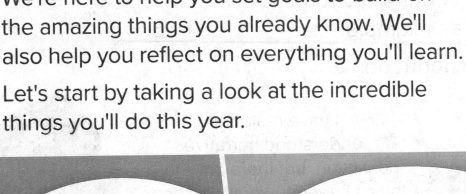

Here's a sneak peek at how you'll do it all.

"Let's go!"

You'll explore new ideas by reading groups of different texts about the same topic. These groups of texts are called *text sets*.

At the beginning of a text set, we'll help you set goals on the My Goals page. You'll see a bar with four boxes beneath each goal. Think about what you already know to fill in the bar. Here's an example.

I can read and understand narrative nonfiction.

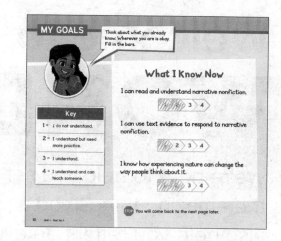

As you move through a text set, you'll explore an essential question and build your knowledge of a topic until you're ready to write about it yourself.

You'll also learn skills that will help you reach your text set goals. At the end of lessons, you'll see a new Check In bar with four boxes.

CHECK IN 1 2 3 4

Reflect on how well you understood a lesson to fill in the bar.

Here are some questions you can ask yourself.

- Was I able to complete the task?

- Was it easy, or was it hard?

- Do I think I need more practice?

At the end of each text set, you'll show off the knowledge you built by completing a fun task. Then you'll return to the second My Goals page where we'll help you reflect on all that you learned.

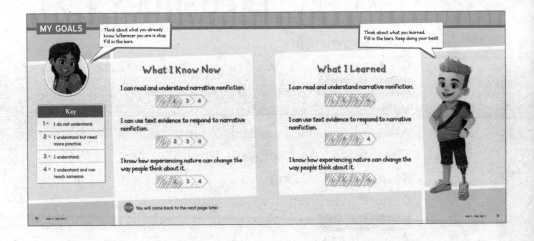

I'll fill in a new set of bars to show how far I've come. I started at 2, but now I'm at 4 because I can read and understand narrative nonfiction well enough to teach a friend.

I'll follow the same steps as I write my own stories, essays, and poems. I own my learning, and you can own yours!

"Let's get started!"

TEXT SET 1 **EXPOSITORY TEXT**

TEXT SET 2 **HISTORICAL FICTION**

Hulton Archive/Getty Images

TEXT SET 3 **ARGUMENTATIVE TEXT**

EXTENDED WRITING

CONNECT AND REFLECT

 Digital Tools

Find this eBook and
other resources at
my.mheducation.com

DanielPrudek/iStock/Getty Images

TEXT SET 1 **HISTORICAL FICTION**

TEXT SET 2 **EXPOSITORY TEXT**

TEXT SET 3 **POETRY**

EXTENDED WRITING

CONNECT AND REFLECT

Digital Tools

Find this eBook and
other resources at
my.mheducation.com

John Robertson/Alamy Stock Photo

Build Knowledge

? Essential Question
How can scientific knowledge change over time?

Build Vocabulary

 Write new words you learned about new technologies that can change scientific knowledge. Draw lines and circles for the words you write.

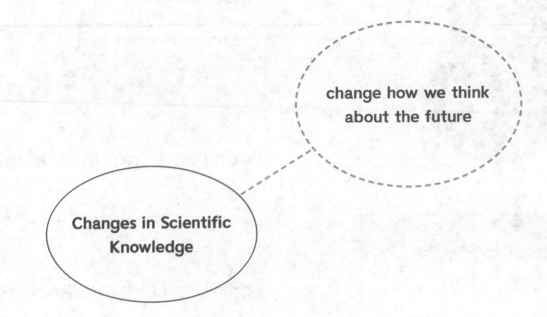

change how we think about the future

Changes in Scientific Knowledge

 Go online to **my.mheducation.com** and read the "A Better World with Satellites" Blast. Think about how scientific knowledge has changed over time. How has new technology affected our world? Then blast back your response.

Think about what you already know. Fill in the bars. You'll learn more with practice.

What I Know Now

Key

1 =	I do not understand.
2 =	I understand but need more practice.
3 =	I understand.
4 =	I understand and can teach someone.

I can read and understand expository text.

1 2 3 4

I can use text evidence to respond to expository text.

1 2 3 4

I know how scientific knowledge changes over time.

1 2 3 4

 **STOP** You will come back to the next page later.

Think about what you learned. Fill in the bars. What is getting easier for you?

What I Learned

I can read and understand expository text.

1 2 3 4

I can use text evidence to respond to expository text.

1 2 3 4

I know how scientific knowledge changes over time.

1 2 3 4

My Goal I can read and understand expository text.

TAKE NOTES

As you read, make note of interesting words and important information.

_____

_____

_____

_____

_____

_____

_____

_____

_____

_____

_____

_____

_____

_____

CHANGING VIEWS OF EARTH

Essential Question

?

How can scientific knowledge change over time?

Read about how our understanding of Earth has changed along with scientific developments over time.

NASA-GFSC Image created by Reto Stockli with the help of Alan Nelson, under the leadership of Fritz Hasler

On the Ground, Looking Around

No matter where on Earth you go, people like to talk about the weather. This weekend's forecast may provide the main **criteria** for planning outdoor activities. Where does all that information about the weather come from? The ability to predict storms and droughts required centuries of scientific innovation. We had to look up at the skies to learn more about life here on Earth.

Long ago, humans based their knowledge on what they experienced with their eyes and ears. If people could heighten their senses, they might not feel so mystified by the events confronting them daily. For example, something as simple as the rising sun perplexed people for centuries. They believed that the Earth stayed in place while the Sun moved around it. This was called the geocentric model.

In the early 1600s, an Italian named Galileo pointed a new tool called the telescope toward the night sky. As a result of his heightened vision, he could see stars, planets, and other celestial **spheres** with new clarity. Each observation and **calculation** led him to support a radical new model of the solar system. In the heliocentric version proposed by the scientist Copernicus, the Sun did not **orbit** the Earth. The Earth orbited the Sun.

Galileo's telescope helped prove that Copernicus's heliocentric view was correct. ▶

These diagrams show the geocentric (Earth in the center), and the heliocentric (Sun in the center) views of the solar system.

Sun
Earth

Earth
Sun

Hulton Archive/Getty Images

FIND TEXT EVIDENCE

> Read

Paragraphs 1–2

Ask and Answer Questions

Why did people long ago think the Sun moved around the Earth? **Underline** the text evidence, and write the answer here.

_____

_____

_____

Paragraph 3

Central Idea and Relevant Details

Look closely at the details in paragraph 3. **Circle** the central idea, or main idea, in this paragraph.

> Reread

Author's Craft

Why was Galileo's use of the telescope so significant?

FIND TEXT EVIDENCE 🔍

Read

Paragraphs 1–2

Ask and Answer Questions

What question do you have about measuring devices? Write your question. **Underline** your answer.

_____

_____

Paragraphs 3–4

Central Idea and Relevant Details

Circle details that support the idea that using aircraft improves how we study weather.

Diagram

At what altitude do the Troposphere and Tropopause meet?

_____

Reread

Author's Craft

Why did the author use the heading "In the Sky, Looking Down" for this section?

In the Sky, Looking Down

New technology allowed scientists to **evaluate** theories better than ever. Measuring devices such as the thermometer and barometer offered new insights into weather patterns. However, people were still limited to ground-based learning. What if they could travel into the sky, where the weather actually happened?

In the mid-1700s, some scientists sent measurement

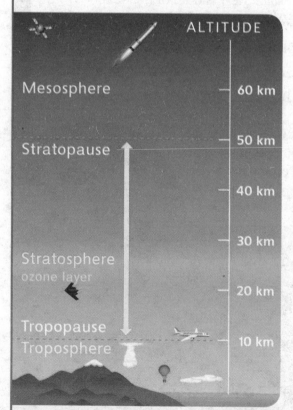

As humans reached higher, we learned more and more about Earth's atmosphere.

devices higher and higher. At first they used kites. Before long, hot-air balloons offered new ways to **transport** the tools—and sometimes scientists themselves—into the sky.

However, scientists were not satisfied studying the lower layers of Earth's atmosphere. The more they learned, the higher they wanted to go. They also wanted to obtain information more quickly and accurately. Kites and balloons were hard to control. As a result, they occasionally veered off course or got lost, taking their data with them.

The development of aircraft in the early 1900s promised safer ways to observe Earth's surface and the atmosphere above it. Kites and balloons could reach altitudes of **approximately** three kilometers. By comparison, airplanes lifted scientists to a height of five kilometers and more. Radio technology allowed scientists to transmit data from the air to the ground, where other scientists analyzed and compared information. Breakthroughs came fast and furiously. Still, scientists dreamed of reaching ever higher.

Out in Space, Looking Back Home

In the late twentieth century, advances in aeronautics led to more powerful rockets that lifted satellites into orbit around Earth. From these heights, scientists could study the composition and relative thinness of our layered atmosphere. Since meteorologists could analyze multiple factors at once, the accuracy of their weather predictions improved dramatically.

NASA launched dozens of satellites into orbit in the following years. Some stared back at Earth, while others peered deep into endless space. They gathered **astronomical** data about the ages of planets and galaxies. Sensors and supercomputers measured things such as Earth's **diameter** with incredible accuracy. Because of this technology, scientists could develop more reliable models about Earth's systems. For example, they could form theories to show how climate might change over time.

Space missions continue to venture farther from home. Even so, nothing compares to seeing Earth the old way, with our own eyes. Views of our planet from space inspire awe in nearly all people who have seen them, even in photographs. "With all the arguments . . . for going to the Moon," said astronaut Joseph Allen, "no one suggested that we should do it to look at the Earth. But that may in fact be the most important reason."

Satellites launched into orbit only last for a limited number of years and then must be replaced.

Summarize

Use your notes and the diagrams, photographs, and captions to write a short summary of the important information in "Changing Views of Earth."

FIND TEXT EVIDENCE

Read
Paragraphs 1–3
Greek Roots

How does the Greek root *photo*, meaning "light," help you understand more about how *photographs* are created?

_____

_____

_____

Evaluate Information

Underline Joseph Allen's quote. Do you think Allen is qualified to say this? Why or why not?

_____

_____

_____

Reread
Author's Craft

Do you believe the ability to predict weather will continue to improve? Why or why not? Use text evidence in your answer.

Vocabulary

Use the example sentences to talk with a partner about each word. Then answer the questions.

approximately

The recipe called for **approximately** two cups of oil, so I did not measure exactly.

What is an antonym, or the opposite, of *approximately*?

_____

_____

astronomical

At the space exhibit, we used **astronomical** instruments to look at the Moon.

What else can you study with astronomical instruments?

_____

_____

calculation

Mina did a **calculation** to see if she had enough money to buy six tickets.

What is one skill that would help with a calculation?

_____

_____

criteria

Blood pressure is one of the **criteria** doctors use to check your health.

What other criteria can doctors use to check your health?

_____

_____

diameter

A large pizza pan has a **diameter** of fourteen inches.

What could you use to measure the diameter of a pan?

_____

_____

Build Your Word List Pick a word you found interesting in the selection you read. Look up synonyms and antonyms of the word in a thesaurus, and write them in your reader's notebook.

evaluate

Reading a food label can help you **evaluate** whether the food has good nutrition.

How can you evaluate a book you have read?

_____

_____

orbit

It takes one year for the Earth to **orbit** the Sun.

What other objects in space orbit the Sun?

_____

_____

_____

spheres

Basketballs and baseballs are **spheres**, but footballs are not.

What other objects are spheres?

_____

_____

_____

Greek Roots

Many English words have Greek roots. The Greek root _geo_ means "earth," so any English word that has the word part _geo_, like _geocentric_, usually has to do with the planet Earth.

🔍 FIND TEXT EVIDENCE

On page 13 of "Changing Views of Earth," I come across the word geocentric. _The Greek root_ centr _means_ "center." _Since I know that_ geo _means_ "earth," _I can figure out that something that is geocentric means "Earth centered." The diagram that shows the Earth in the center with the Sun and planets traveling around it must be the_ geocentric _model._

They believed that the Earth stayed in place while the Sun moved around it. This was called the geocentric model.

Your Turn Use the Greek roots below to figure out the meanings of two words from "Changing Views of Earth."

Greek Roots: helio = sun   therm = heat
          meter = measure

heliocentric, _page 13_ _____

thermometer, _page 14_ _____

CHECK IN 1 2 3 4

Ask and Answer Questions

Asking and answering questions as you read helps you to deepen your understanding of the text. Try it with "Changing Views of Earth." Think about each question the author asks, and generate your own questions, too. Then read on for the answers. After you have finished reading, think about more questions related to the topic that you might have.

 FIND TEXT EVIDENCE

In the first paragraph on page 13, the author asks a question:

Where does all that information about the weather come from? This may lead you to another question.

Page 13

No matter where on Earth you go, people like to talk about the weather. This weekend's forecast may provide the main **criteria** for planning outdoor activities. Where does all that information about the weather come from?

I think about what I already know—that weather forecasters use scientific instruments. So I ask myself, "What kinds of instruments do scientists use to make forecasts?" I will read on to find the answer.

 Your Turn Reread "Out in Space, Looking Back Home" on page 15. Ask a question and then read to find the answer. Use the strategy Ask and Answer Questions as you read. Write your question and answer below.

_____

_____

CHECK IN ⟩ 1 ⟩ 2 ⟩ 3 ⟩ 4 ⟩

Diagrams

The selection "Changing Views of Earth" is an expository text. Expository text presents and structures information and facts about a topic in a logical order. It often includes a variety of text structures to support points with reasons and evidence. It may also include text features, such as subheadings, photos, diagrams, and captions.

Readers to Writers

Writers use diagrams to illustrate important information in the text. When might you use a diagram in your own writing?

FIND TEXT EVIDENCE

"Changing Views of Earth" is an expository text. The facts about inventions are given in a chronological order. The author backs up her points with evidence, including diagrams.

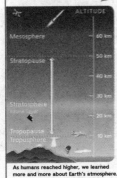

Page 14

In the Sky, Looking Down

New technology allowed scientists to **evaluate** theories better than ever. Measuring devices such as the thermometer and barometer offered new insights into weather patterns. However, people were still limited to ground-based learning. What if they could travel into the sky, where the weather actually happened?

In the mid-1700s, some scientists sent measurement devices higher and higher. At first they used kites. Before long, hot-air balloons offered new ways to **transport** the tools—and sometimes scientists themselves—into the sky.

However, scientists were not satisfied studying the lower layers of Earth's atmosphere. The more they learned, the higher they wanted to go. They also wanted to obtain information more quickly and accurately. Kites and balloons were hard to control. As a result, they occasionally veered off course or got lost, taking their data with them.

The development of aircraft in the early 1900s promised safer ways to observe Earth's surface and the atmosphere above it. Kites and balloons could reach altitudes of **approximately** three kilometers. By comparison, airplanes lifted scientists to a height of five kilometers and more. Radio technology allowed scientists to transmit data from the air to the ground, where other scientists analyzed and compared information. Breakthroughs came fast and furiously. Still, scientists dreamed of reaching ever higher.

As humans reached higher, we learned more and more about Earth's atmosphere.

Diagrams

A diagram is a drawing that shows the different parts of something and how the parts relate to one another. Labels identify different parts of the diagram.

Your Turn Review and discuss why "Changing Views of Earth" is an expository text. How is the information in the two diagrams helpful?

_____

_____

_____

_____

CHECK IN 1 2 3 4

Central Idea and Relevant Details

A **central idea**, or main idea, is what expository authors want readers to know most about a topic. Each text has a central idea, but each section or paragraph has its own central idea. To determine the central idea, look closely at relevant details such as facts and examples. These details convey important information about the central idea.

🔍 FIND TEXT EVIDENCE

In the section "On the Ground, Looking Around" on page 13, I read details about how people used different ways to view the sky. These details are relevant because they support the idea that people used different methods over time. I can find the central idea.

Central Idea
People made new discoveries about the Earth's model as methods became more advanced.
Detail
For many years, people only had eyes to view the sky. They proposed the geocentric model. They supported this model with evidence they saw with their eyes.
Detail
The telescope was invented. Scientists saw the stars and planets more closely.
Detail
Galileo used the telescope to observe and test ideas. His careful work led him to support a different model. He proved that Copernicus's heliocentric model was correct.

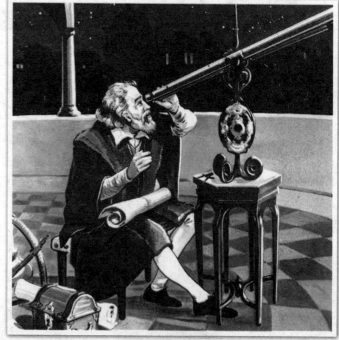

Your Turn Reread the selection "Changing Views of Earth." Record the central idea and relevant details in your graphic organizer on page 21.

CHECK IN ▷ 1 ▷ 2 ▷ 3 ▷ 4 ▷

Hulton Archive/Getty Images

Central Idea
Detail
Detail
Detail

Respond to Reading

Discuss the prompt below. Use your notes and text evidence to support your answer.

COLLABORATE

What is the author's purpose for providing an in-depth look at the chronology of our study of Earth and space?

_____

_____

_____

_____

_____

_____

_____

_____

_____

_____

_____

_____

_____

Quick Tip

Use these sentence starters to discuss the text and to organize ideas.

- *The author uses text structure to . . .*
- *The author includes text features that . . .*
- *The author ends with . . .*

Grammar Connections

Irregular verbs do not form the past by adding *d* or *ed*. As you write your response, make sure to use irregular verbs correctly. For instance:

*This observation **led** scientists to . . .*

*In the mid-1700s, some scientists **sent** . . .*

CHECK IN 1 2 3 4

Scientific Knowledge Grows

COLLABORATE

As scientists improved technology over time, their ideas about the solar system changed. Create a podcast that explains the relationship of the Earth, Sun, and Moon. Work collaboratively in a larger group.

Step 1 **Set a Goal** Focus your search. Write your topic below.

_____

Step 2 **Identify Sources** Discuss the reliable print or online sources you might use to research.

Step 3 **Find and Record Information** As you take notes, make sure to cite the information properly. **Paraphrasing** means using your own words to restate the source's information. The meaning of the information stays the same. **Plagiarism** is copying an author's exact words and using them as your own. Avoid plagiarism by paraphrasing a source. If you quote an author's exact words, cite the source. Here is an example: On page 14 of "Changing Views of Earth" the text states, "Kites and balloons were hard to control." Paraphrase this quote.

_____

_____

Step 4 **Organize and Synthesize Information** Organize your notes to draft your podcast. Do not plagiarize any information.

Step 5 **Create and Present** Complete your podcast. After you finish, present your work to the class. Tell what your sources are at the end of the podcast.

---

original text

The ability to predict storms and droughts required centuries of scientific innovation.

paraphrased text

It took hundreds of years of testing new ideas and tools to accurately forecast the weather correctly.

How is the second text a paraphrase of the original?

_____

_____

_____

_____

_____

CHECK IN ⟩ 1 ⟩ 2 ⟩ 3 ⟩ 4

When Is a Planet Not a Planet?

Literature Anthology:
pages 346–361

 How does the author use the first part of "Pluto's Problems" to support her ideas about Pluto?

Talk About It Reread **Literature Anthology** page 349. Turn to a partner and discuss how the information in the section is organized.

Cite Text Evidence What information does the author want you to know about the planets? Write text evidence in the chart.

Synthesize Information

Combine what you already know about planets with the information in the text in order to better understand the ideas the author is presenting. Remember to also look at the information in the illustrations and captions.

Inner Planets	Outer Planets

Write The author supports her ideas about Pluto by _____

_____

_____

_____

CHECK IN ⟩ 1 ⟩ 2 ⟩ 3 ⟩ 4 ⟩

Look at the photos and reread the caption. What do you notice about the size of the telescope? Why do you think having such a large telescope is necessary to studying space?

 Talk About It **Literature Anthology** page 356. Turn to a partner, and discuss what you learned from the photographs and caption.

Cite Text Evidence Why might such large telescopes be needed to study space? Write text evidence in the chart.

Quick Tip

Use these sentence starters to talk about the photographs and caption.

• *The photographs help me see . . .*

• *I know that Pluto . . .*

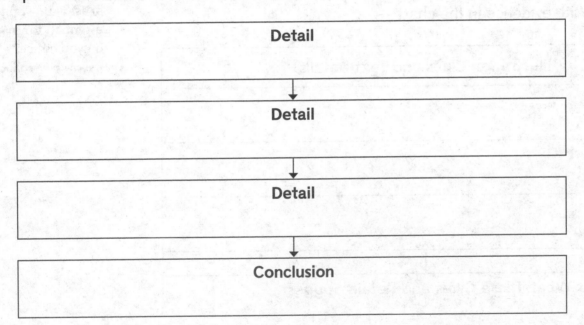

Detail

↓

Detail

↓

Detail

↓

Conclusion

Write Having such a large telescope is necessary to study space because

_____

_____

_____

CHECK IN 1 ⟩ 2 ⟩ 3 ⟩ 4

Study the author's rendering and read the caption. What advantages might an unmanned spacecraft have in discovering new information?

Talk About It Reread **Literature Anthology** page 360. Turn to a partner and discuss what you learned from this rendering and caption.

Cite Text Evidence What do you learn from the illustration clues and text details about how an unmanned spacecraft might help find new discoveries? Write evidence in the chart.

Reread **Literature Anthology** page 360.

Illustration Clues and Text Details

↓

What These Clues and Details Suggest

Write The advantages that an unmanned spacecraft might have in discovering new information are that _____

_____

_____

Quick Tip

When you look at artists' renderings, think about why an artist might have chosen to illustrate this particular scene. What would be the artist's purpose for illustrating this scene? What might the artist want you to pay attention to? What details do you notice?

CHECK IN ⟩ 1 ⟩ 2 ⟩ 3 ⟩ 4 ⟩

Respond to Reading

COLLABORATE

Discuss the prompt below. Use your notes and text evidence to support your response.

The author says that "new information is just waiting to be discovered." What kind of technology seems most useful for finding information about the universe? Support your answer with text evidence.

_____

_____

_____

_____

_____

_____

_____

_____

_____

_____

_____

Quick Tip

Use these sentence starters to talk about and cite text evidence.

- *Technology that has helped astronomers includes . . .*

- *The most important kind of technology includes . . .*

- *Benefits of this technology include . . .*

CHECK IN 1 2 3 4

The Crow and the Pitcher

Literature Anthology: pages 364–365

1   *A fable is a form of classical literature that usually includes animals as characters and ends with a moral. Aesop was an ancient Greek storyteller who is credited with many fables, now known as Aesop's Fables. His criteria for a good tale seem simple: Tell a meaningful story and end with an unforgettable moral.*

2   A crow, whose throat was parched and dry with thirst, saw a pitcher in the distance. With great joy, he flew to it.

3   The crow found that the pitcher held a little water.

4   He stooped and he strained, but the water was too near the bottom of the pitcher. He could not reach it.

5   Next he tried to overturn the pitcher, thinking that he would be able to catch some of the water as it trickled out.

Reread paragraphs 2, 3, and 4. **Circle** the text evidence that explains the crow's problem. Write your answer here:

_____

_____

_____

_____

_____

_____

COLLABORATE

Discuss with a partner what the crow did to try to solve his problem. **Underline** the crow's attempts. Talk about what you think the crow might do next.

6   The tired crow was too weak to knock over the pitcher. He took a minute to evaluate the situation and devise a plan.

7   He collected as many stones as he could.

8   He dropped a stone into the pitcher with his beak. Then he peered into the pitcher.

9   He could not tell if his plan was working yet, so he dropped another stone into the pitcher. And then he added another.

10   The crow looked again. "This experiment just might work!" he thought.

11   One by one the crow dropped stones into the pitcher until he brought the water within his reach and thus saved his life.

12   Moral: *Necessity is the mother of invention.*

Reread the text. **Make marks** next to the additional steps the crow took to save himself.

COLLABORATE

Reread the moral of the fable. Discuss with your partner what you think it means. Write your ideas below.

_____

_____

_____

_____

_____

_____

_____

? How do the crow's actions help convey the author's message?

COLLABORATE

Talk About It Reread the excerpts on pages 28 and 29.

Discuss the crow's problem and the moral of the fable.

Cite Text Evidence What do the crow's actions show? Write the text evidence in the chart.

Evaluate Information

Reread paragraph 1 on page 28. Think about the characteristics of a fable. Discuss with your partner how "The Crow and the Pitcher" fits these characteristics.

Beginning	Middle	End

What It Shows

Write The crow's actions convey the author's message by _____

_____

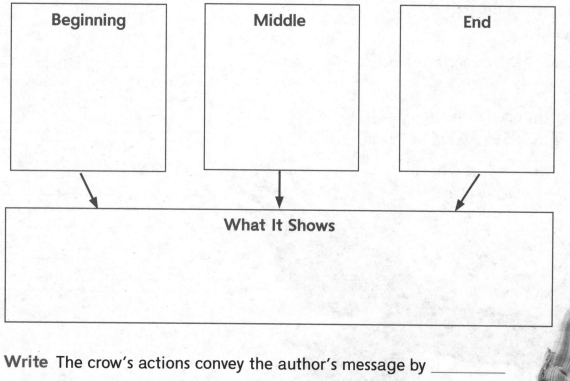

CHECK IN ▷ 1 ▷ 2 ▷ 3 ▷ 4

Imagery

Writers use imagery to help create mental images in a reader's mind. These words and phrases often appeal to the senses to describe what something looks, smells, feels, tastes, and sounds like. Imagery can also affect mood, or the feeling, the writer creates in the reader.

 FIND TEXT EVIDENCE

On page 28 of "The Crow and the Pitcher" in paragraph 2, the author says that the crow's throat was "parched and dry with thirst." By using this phrase, the author creates an image that helps readers imagine how their throats would feel if they were suffering from extreme thirst.

> A crow, whose throat was parched and dry with thirst, saw a pitcher in the distance.

 Your Turn Reread the rest of page 28 and paragraph 6 on page 29.

- What words does the author use to create imagery? _____

  _____

- How does the author's use of imagery create and maintain the mood of

  the story? _____

  _____

Readers to Writers

You can use imagery in your writing. Think about what you want your readers to see, hear, touch, smell, or taste. Choose words that create these images. Also think about the mood of your writing. If you want a scary, calm, anxious, or happy mood, choose words and phrases that help to set and maintain this mood.

CHECK IN 1 > 2 > 3 > 4 >

? How do the artist and the authors of *When Is a Planet Not a Planet?* and "The Crow and the Pitcher" help you understand how knowledge can be gained?

Talk About It Look at the painting. Read the caption. Talk with a partner about what you see in the painting.

Cite Text Evidence Circle what the artist wants you to focus on. Think about how and why people gain knowledge. Reread the caption and **underline** evidence that helps you understand how a comet inspired scientific knowledge.

Write The artist and authors show how knowledge can be gained by

_____

_____

_____

_____

_____

_____

William Turner of Oxford/Yale Center for British Art, Paul Mellon Collection.

Giovanni Battista Donati discovered this comet over Florence, Italy, on June 2, 1858. It was observed and studied by many astronomers. The comet became the subject of newspaper and magazine articles. William Turner's painting captures the comet's curved tail. Donati's comet inspired many scientists and people to learn more about the night sky.

Quick Tip

Think about what you have read in the selections and in the caption on this page. Talk about how knowledge is gained and what makes people want to gain knowledge.

CHECK IN 1 2 3 4

Write a Report

Think about what you learned about how we gain scientific knowledge. Why are scientists inspired to conduct new experiments or improve technology?

1 Look at your Build Knowledge notes in your reader's notebook.

2 Make a list of the ways scientists are inspired. Use evidence from the texts you read to support your ideas.

3 Use your ideas to write a report about why it is important to conduct experiments or improve technology even when we know something to be proven. Use the new vocabulary words you learned.

Think about what you learned in this text set. Fill in the bars on page 11.

? Essential Question

How do shared experiences help people adapt to change?

Build Vocabulary

Write new words you learned about how people can adapt to change. Draw lines and circles for the words you write.

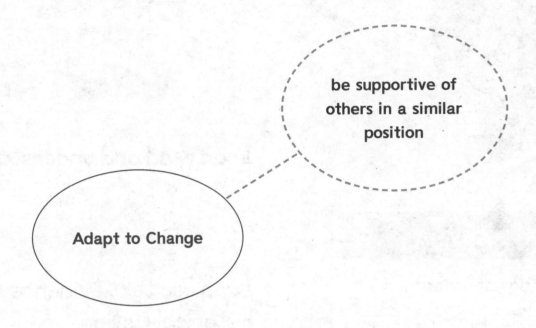

Adapt to Change

be supportive of others in a similar position

Go online to **my.mheducation.com** and read the "Shared Experiences" Blast. Think about how shared experiences help people adapt to change. How might music help people come together during times of change? Then blast back your response.

Think about what you already know. Fill in the bars. Keep doing your best!

What I Know Now

Key

1 =	I do not understand.
2 =	I understand but need more practice.
3 =	I understand.
4 =	I understand and can teach someone.

I can read and understand historical fiction.

$$1 > 2 > 3 > 4$$

I can use text evidence to respond to historical fiction.

$$1 > 2 > 3 > 4$$

I know how sharing experiences helps people change.

$$1 > 2 > 3 > 4$$

STOP You will come back to the next page later.

Think about what you learned. Fill in the bars. You can always improve, so keep trying!

What I Learned

I can read and understand historical fiction.

1 > 2 > 3 > 4

I can use text evidence to respond to historical fiction.

1 > 2 > 3 > 4

I know how sharing experiences helps people change.

1 > 2 > 3 > 4

TAKE NOTES

As you read, make note of interesting words and important events.

_____

_____

_____

_____

_____

_____

_____

_____

_____

_____

_____

_____

_____

The Day the Rollets Got Their Moxie Back

Essential Question

?

How do shared experiences help people adapt to change?

Read about how a family comes together during a period of great hardship in the United States.

Ron Mazellan

Sometimes, the thing that gets you through hard times comes like a bolt from the blue. That's what my older brother's letter was like, traveling across the country from a work camp in Wyoming. It was 1937, and Ricky was helping to build facilities for a new state park as part of President Roosevelt's employment program. Though the program created jobs for young men like Ricky, it hadn't helped our dad find work yet.

I imagined Ricky looking up at snowcapped mountains and sparkling skies, breathing in the smell of evergreens as his work crew turned trees into lumber and lumber into buildings. It almost made an 11-year-old **weakling** like me want to become a lumberjack.

Back in our New York City apartment, the air smelled like meatloaf and cabbage. Dad sat slantwise in his chair by the window, **obviously** trying to catch the last rays of sunlight rather than turn on a light. My older sister Ruth and I lay on the floor comparing the letters Ricky had sent us.

"Shirley, Ricky says they had a talent show, and he wore a grass skirt and did a hula dance while playing the ukulele!" Ruth reported with delight. "I'll bet he was the cat's pajamas!"

"It'd be swell to have our own talent show!" I replied.

"Should I start sewing grass skirts?" Mom asked from the kitchen, which was just the corner where someone had plopped down a stove next to a sink and an icebox. "Now come set the table. Dinner's almost ready."

FIND TEXT EVIDENCE 🔍

Read

Paragraphs 1–6
Make Predictions

Make a prediction based on the girls' conversation. Write the text evidence for your prediction.

_____

_____

_____

Paragraph 5
Plot: Characterization

Underline the example of dialect in paragaph 5. What does this reveal about Shirley's character?

_____

Reread
Author's Craft

What point of view is the story written from? Why might the author have written the story from this point of view?

FIND TEXT EVIDENCE

Read

Paragraphs 1–3

Plot: Conflict

Compare and contrast the characters' attitudes at the dinner table. **Circle** words and phrases you used as clues. What are their attitudes?

_____

_____

_____

Paragraph 4

Idioms

What clues in the text help you to understand the meaning of "grin and bear it"?

_____

_____

_____

Reread

Author's Craft

What message is the author sending by showing how the family responds to their troubles?

Dad stayed where he was, sullen and spent. "Any jobs in the paper?" Mom asked, her voice rich with **sympathy**. Dad shook his head no. He had worked as an artist in the theater for years, but most productions were still strapped for cash. Dad sketched posters for shows that did get the green light, just to keep his skills sharp. He even designed posters for "Rollet's Follies" with Ruth and me depicted in watercolor costumes.

For dinner, Mom served a baked loaf of whatever ingredients she had that worked well together. From the reddish color, I could **assume** that she had snuck in beets. "I **guarantee** you'll like these beets," she said, reading my frown. "It's beet loaf, the meatless meat loaf," she sang as she served up slices.

Ruth fidgeted in her seat, still excited about the talent show. Though calm on the outside, inside I was all atwitter, too.

Over the next week, Ruth and I practiced our Hawaiian dance routine. Our parents worried about heating bills as cold weather settled in. One Saturday, my father decided to grin and bear it and grab some hot coffee at the local soup kitchen, where he hoped to hear about available jobs. Ruth and I begged to go along. Since the kitchen offered doughnuts and hot chocolate on weekends, he agreed.

Ron Mazellan

Most everyone in line was bundled up against the cold. Many of us had to **rely** on two or three threadbare layers. Like many other men, Dad bowed his head as if in shame.

The line moved slowly. Bored, Ruth began practicing her dance steps. I sang an upbeat tune to give her some music. Around us, downturned hats lifted to reveal frowns becoming smiles. Soon, folks began clapping along. Egged on by the **supportive** response, Ruth twirled and swayed like there was no tomorrow.

"Those girls sure have moxie!" someone shouted.

"They've got heart, all right!" offered another. "Why, they oughta be in pictures!"

"With performances like that, I'd **nominate** them for an Academy Award!" a woman called out.

"Those are my girls!" Dad declared, his head held high.

Everyone burst into applause. For those short moments, the past didn't matter, and the future blossomed ahead of us like a beautiful flower. I couldn't wait to write Ricky and tell him the news.

Summarize

Use your notes to orally summarize the plot and theme of this story.

FIND TEXT EVIDENCE

Read

Paragraphs 1–2
Plot: Conflict
Underline the words that show how the people's mood changes.

Paragraphs 3-7
Confirm Predictions
How accurate was your prediction?

_____

_____

_____

_____

_____

_____

_____

_____

Reread
Author's Craft

How does the author use imagery to show the father has changed by the end of the story?

Vocabulary

Use the example sentences to talk with a partner about each word. Then answer the questions.

assume

Caitlyn could only **assume** the cat had broken the flowerpot since Pip was standing over the pieces.

What might you assume if you awaken to a major snowstorm on a school day?

_____

_____

guarantee

The weather forecaster can **guarantee** that it will rain soon because of the dark clouds approaching.

When else might you guarantee something?

_____

_____

nominate

The team will **nominate** the best candidate for team captain.

When might you nominate a particular person for a task or position?

_____

_____

obviously

The scarf was **obviously** too long for Marta.

What clothes are obviously wrong for a cold day?

_____

_____

rely

Calvin must **rely** on his notes in order to study.

When have you had to rely on someone else?

_____

_____

Build Your Word List Circle the word *supportive* on page 41. In your reader's notebook, list its root word and related words. Then do the same with another word that uses the suffix *-ive*. Use an online or print dictionary to find more related words.

supportive

The audience's **supportive** applause boosted Clare's energy as she played her violin.

How else can you be supportive of a performer onstage?

_____

_____

_____

sympathy

Jamar's dad gave him **sympathy** when his team lost the game.

When else might you express sympathy to someone?

_____

_____

_____

weakling

Being sick in bed made Emily feel like a **weakling**.

Why might being sick make someone feel like a weakling?

_____

_____

Idioms

An **idiom** is an expression that uses words in a creative way. Surrounding words and sentences can help you understand the meaning of an idiom.

🔍 FIND TEXT EVIDENCE

I'm not sure what the idiom a bolt from the blue means on page 39. When I think of a "bolt," I think of lightning and how quickly and unpredictably it can strike. Letters often come unexpectedly, as if out of nowhere. That must be the meaning.

Sometimes, the thing that gets you through hard times comes like a bolt from the blue. That's what my older brother's letter was like, traveling across the country from a work camp in Wyoming.

Your Turn Use context clues to explain the meanings of the following idioms from "The Day the Rollets Got Their Moxie Back."

the cat's pajamas, *page 39* _____

get the green light, *page 40* _____

_____

CHECK IN 1 2 3 4

Make Predictions

Making predictions helps you read with purpose. As you read a story, illustrations and clues in the text can help you predict what will happen next. Understanding the characteristics of a genre can also help inform your prediction. As you continue to read, you can confirm if your predictions are correct.

🔍 **FIND TEXT EVIDENCE**

You can make predictions about the story "The Day the Rollets Got Their Moxie Back," beginning with the genre label and the title.

Page 38

The Day the Rollets Got Their Moxie Back

Essential Question

? How do shared experiences help people adapt to change?

Read about how a family comes together during a period of great hardship in the United States.

From the title, I predict that the main characters in the historical fiction story will be the Rollets. The story will probably have a positive ending since the Rollets will get back something that they have been missing.

Your Turn Use the illustration and the last paragraph on page 40 to discuss a prediction readers might make about the story.

_____

_____

_____

_____

CHECK IN 1 2 3 4

Plot: Characterization

"The Day the Rollets Got Their Moxie Back" is historical fiction. It features events and settings typical of the time in which the story takes place. It also features characters' dialect, which is acting and speaking like people from a certain place in the past. Analyzing the characters' dialect can help you know what they learn and how they change throughout the story.

FIND TEXT EVIDENCE

"The Day the Rollets Got Their Moxie Back" is historical fiction. The year is 1937, and President Roosevelt was real. The Rollets use dialect of the time.

Readers to Writers

Dialect is not only associated with history, but is also related to certain places. For example, people from the West might have different sayings from those in the South. Are there any sayings specific to where you live?

Page 39

Sometimes, the thing that gets you through hard times comes like a bolt from the blue. That's what my older brother's letter was like, traveling across the country from a work camp in Wyoming. It was 1937, and Ricky was helping to build facilities for a new state park as part of President Roosevelt's employment program. Though the program created jobs for young men like Ricky, it hadn't helped our dad find work yet.

I imagined Ricky looking up at snow-capped mountains and sparkling skies, breathing in the smell of evergreens as his work crew turned trees into lumber and lumber into buildings. It almost made an 11-year-old weakling like me want to become a lumberjack.

Back in our New York City apartment, the air smelled like meatloaf and cabbage. Dad sat slant-wise in his chair by the window, obviously trying to catch the last rays of sunlight rather than turn on a light. My older sister Ruth and I lay on the floor comparing the letters Ricky had sent us.

"Shirley, Ricky says they had a talent show, and he wore a grass skirt and did a hula dance while playing the ukulele!" Ruth reported with delight. "I'll bet he was the cat's pajamas!"

"It'd be swell to have our own talent show!" I replied.

"Should I start sewing grass skirts?" Mom asked from the kitchen, which was just the corner where someone had plopped down a stove next to a sink and an icebox. "Now come set the table. Dinner's almost ready."

Dialect

Dialect is a form of characterization. It may include unfamiliar words, phrases, or idioms. It can reveal how the characters feel or what they think about an idea.

COLLABORATE

Your Turn List another example of dialect in "The Day the Rollets Got Their Moxie Back." Why might an author include dialect in historical fiction?

_____

_____

_____

_____

CHECK IN 1 > 2 > 3 > 4

Plot: Conflict

When you compare and contrast the characters' personalities and actions in a story, you can better understand how they respond to the conflict, or problem. Knowing how the characters respond to the conflict helps you analyze how the plot advances, or moves forward.

Quick Tip

Comparing and contrasting the characters' speech, feelings, motivations, and interactions can help you better understand their responses to the conflict.

🔍 FIND TEXT EVIDENCE

When I reread page 40 of "The Day the Rollets Got Their Moxie Back," I compare the family members' personalities and actions to determine how they respond to the conflict and how the conflict affects the story.

Dad
Dad is sullen. He is quiet at dinner.

Mom
Mother is sympathetic to Dad. She tries to cheer him up.

How does the conflict affect the story?
Each character is affected by Dad losing his job. The plot advances by how the characters respond to the conflict.

Ruth
Ruth fidgets but is excited about putting on a talent show for fun.

Shirley
Shirley frowns at their dinner but is excited about the talent show, too.

Your Turn Compare the characters' actions and responses at the soup kitchen. Fill in the graphic organizer on page 47.

CHECK IN ▶ 1 ▶ 2 ▶ 3 ▶ 4

Ron Mazellan

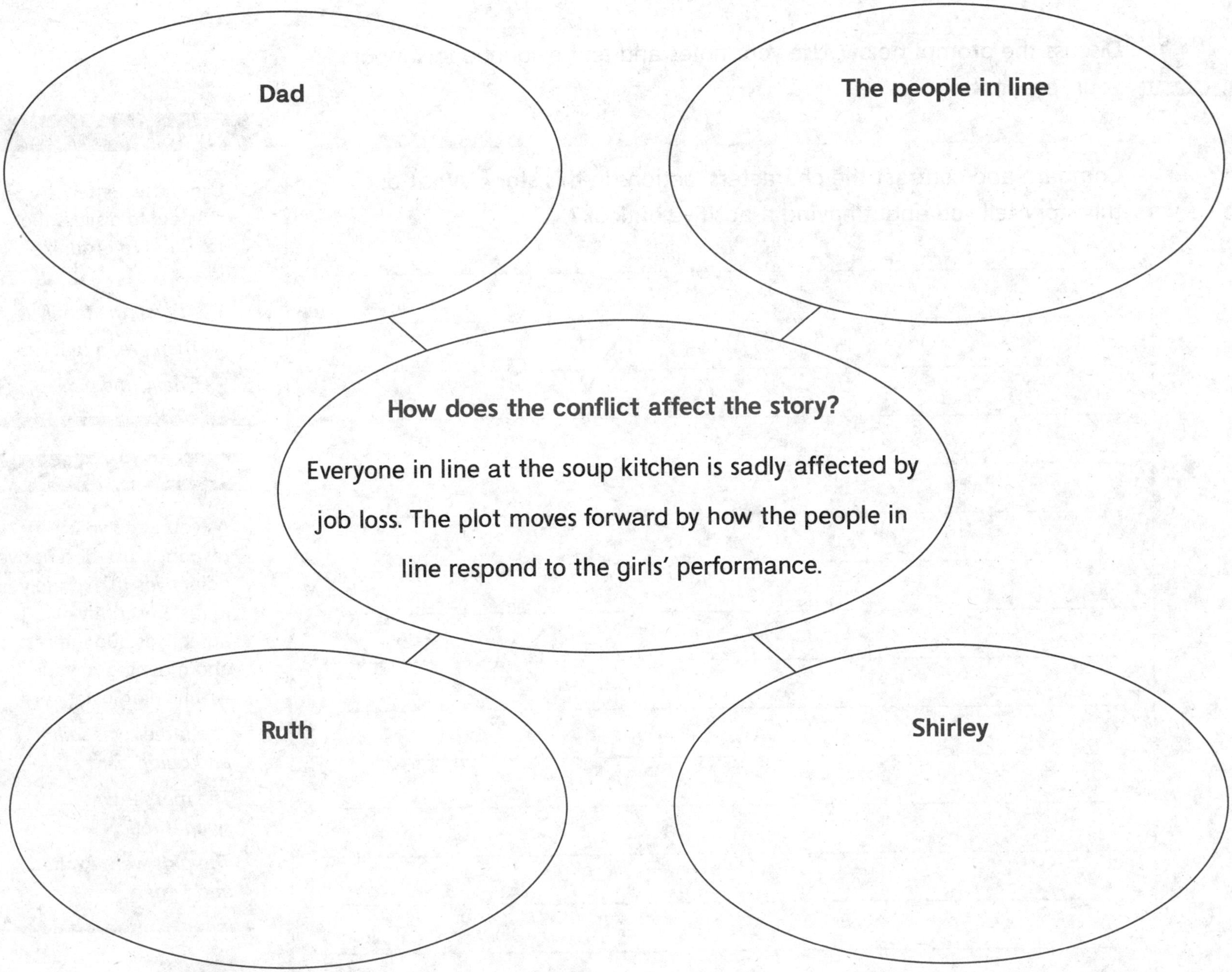

Dad

The people in line

How does the conflict affect the story?

Everyone in line at the soup kitchen is sadly affected by job loss. The plot moves forward by how the people in line respond to the girls' performance.

Ruth

Shirley

Respond to Reading

COLLABORATE Discuss the prompt below. Use your notes and text evidence to support your response.

Compare and contrast the characters' actions in this story. What does this story tell you about having a positive outlook?

_____

_____

_____

_____

_____

_____

_____

_____

_____

_____

_____

_____

_____

_____

Quick Tip

Use these sentence starters to discuss the text and to organize ideas.

- *At first, the family is . . .*
- *Then I read that . . .*
- *Finally, the girls . . .*

Grammar Connections

As you write your response, use descriptive adjectives to expand your ideas. Descriptive adjectives add interest and meaning to your writing. For instance:

*The father was **sullen** and **quiet**.*

*The mother was **sympathetic**.*

*The girls were **excited** and **fidgety**.*

CHECK IN 1 2 3 4

Supporting One Another

For many people, experiencing hard times together reminds them that they share things in common. Follow the research process to create a collage about the experiences people encountered during the Great Depression. Work collaboratively with a partner.

Step 1 **Set a Goal** Narrow your search. Write your topic below.

_____

Step 2 **Identify Sources** Discuss the print or online sources you will use to research. Make sure they are credible, or trustworthy, primary and secondary sources. When evaluating sources, ask yourself:

- Is the source identified and well-known for accuracy?
- Is the information in the source well organized?
- Is information documented and credited?

What can you do to check if an online source is credible?

_____

_____

Step 3 **Find and Record Information** Take notes. Cite your sources when you include specific examples of photos, art, or text.

Step 4 **Organize and Synthesize Information** Organize your notes. Decide how you want to create your collage. Plan on the photos, art, or text you will include.

Step 5 **Create and Present** Complete your collage. After you finish, present your work to the class.

Tech Tip

Ask your teacher or another adult to recommend collage-maker programs you can use. Many programs will allow you to shape your collage and add text, labels, and backgrounds as well as photos and art.

Why is a library a good place to find credible sources? What are some examples of credible sources you might use?

_____

_____

_____

_____

_____

CHECK IN 1 2 3 4

Bud, Not Buddy

 What does the author reveal about Bud through his responses to the conversation he overhears?

Literature Anthology: pages 366–379

Talk About It Reread **Literature Anthology** pages 368–369. Discuss with your partner what Bud thinks and does. Discuss why he reacts in this way.

Cite Text Evidence What does Bud do after he overhears the conversation? Write text evidence in the chart.

 Evaluate Information

Looking at what a character says and does can help you evaluate the character's behavior and analyze his or her relationship with other characters. Evaluate the things Bud does after he overhears the conversation. How does this help you understand how the author wants readers to feel about Bud?

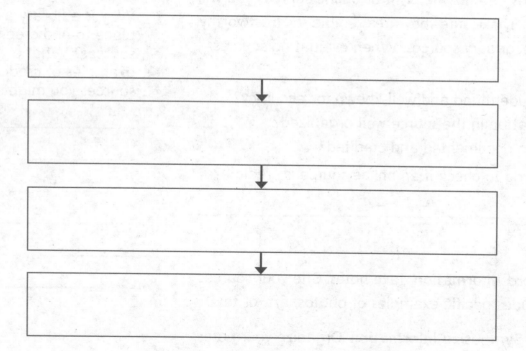

Write The author helps me know more about Bud by _____

_____

CHECK IN 1 2 3 4

How does the author show how Bud will have to change to stay with the band?

Talk About It Reread **Literature Anthology** page 372. Turn to your partner, and discuss what Bud is expected to do. Discuss specific ideas in the text that are important to the meaning.

Cite Text Evidence How is what Bud is expected to do different from what he is used to? Write text evidence in the chart.

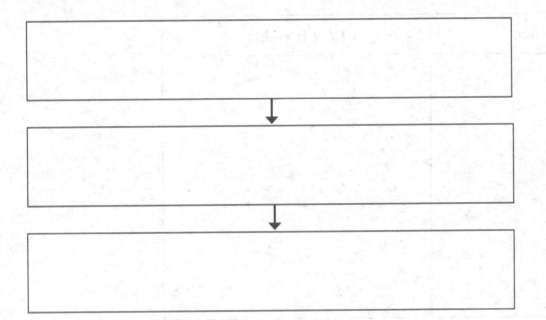

Write The author helps me understand how Bud will have to change by

_____

_____

_____

CHECK IN 1 > 2 > 3 > 4

? **How does the author help you understand how Bud changes as he becomes part of the band?**

Talk About It Reread **Literature Anthology** page 378. Turn to a partner and discuss how Bud feels about his new nickname and what he is expected to do. Evaluate details in the story to determine important ideas.

Cite Text Evidence What words and phrases help you see how Bud changes? Write text evidence.

Text Evidence	How It Helps

Write I understand how Bud changes because the author _____

_____

_____

Quick Tip

Rereading can help you think about why characters act a certain way. How does Bud act when he hears his new name?

CHECK IN ⟩ 1 ⟩ 2 ⟩ 3 ⟩ 4 ⟩

Respond to Reading

COLLABORATE Discuss the prompt below. Use your notes and text evidence to support your ideas.

What is the meaning behind Bud's original set of rules? How do they affect Bud's experiences as the story progresses?

_____

_____

_____

_____

_____

_____

_____

_____

_____

_____

_____

Quick Tip

Use these sentence starters to talk about and cite text evidence.

• *The rules change . . .*

• *This is important because . . .*

• *This affects the story . . .*

Photo Spin/Getty Images

CHECK IN 1 2 3 4

Musical Impressions of the Great Depression

Literature Anthology: pages 382–385

Sympathy Through Song

1   Many songs of the 1930s, particularly in folk and country music, recounted people's stories of loss and hardship. The songwriter Woody Guthrie followed farm workers who traveled west to California hoping to find work. He saw that they often encountered new and tougher challenges. Guthrie expressed sympathy for them through songs like "Dust Bowl Blues" and "Goin' Down the Road Feeling Bad." He hoped to restore people's sense of dignity.

2   Meanwhile, across the country, the Carter Family performed similar songs, such as "Worried Man Blues," describing life in the Appalachian Mountains where resources were scarce. Listeners found comfort in the knowledge that they were not alone in their struggles.

Reread the excerpt. Evaluate details to determine important ideas. **Underline** the sentence that explains the goal of Woody Guthrie's music. Write how this kind of music affected people who struggled during this time.

_____

_____

_____

_____

COLLABORATE

Talk with your partner about why music was able to change how people felt during a difficult time. **Circle** text evidence in the excerpt.

On the Up-Swing

[3]   Times were certainly hard in the country. In the nation's cities, the situation was equally difficult. In some African American communities, unemployment soared above fifty percent. These challenges reminded some of earlier times of slavery, and many found comfort in the musical styles of that era: gospel and blues.

[4]   Jazz, a newer form of music with upbeat rhythms, lifted people's spirits. Band leaders like Duke Ellington and Count Basie created a new, high-energy style of jazz called swing. Around the country, people of all races responded to these positive rhythms. People left their problems behind and escaped onto the dance floor.

[5]   In New York, Broadway musicals delighted theatergoers. Many musicals offered light entertainment, while others addressed the current hardships through songs, such as "Brother, Can You Spare a Dime?" Radio helped spread these songs beyond the city, connecting people across the country and creating nationwide hits.

Reread paragraphs 3 and 4. **Circle** examples of music that affected people.

COLLABORATE

With a partner, talk about how the author describes the different kinds of music.

Underline a sentence in paragraph 5 that describes another kind of music that affected people.

Why is "On the Up-Swing" a good heading for this section? Evaluate details and use text evidence to support your answer.

_____

_____

_____

_____

_____

_____

_____

? **What is the author's purpose for writing this selection?**

COLLABORATE

Talk About It Reread the excerpts on pages 54 and 55. Discuss what the author wants you to know about music during the Great Depression.

Cite Text Evidence What words and phrases tell you why the author wrote this selection? Write text evidence in the chart.

Clues	Author's Purpose

Write The author's purpose for writing this selection was _____

_____

_____

_____

_____

CHECK IN ⟩ 1 ⟩ 2 ⟩ 3 ⟩ 4 ⟩

Compare and Contrast

When authors use a compare-and-contrast text structure, they show how ideas can be alike and different while supporting a central, or main, idea. Authors use signal words and phrases, such as *however*, *while*, or *similarly*.

FIND TEXT EVIDENCE

On page 55 in paragraph 5, the author compares and contrasts how Broadway musicals helped people through hard times. The word *while* is a clue that something is being compared.

> In New York, Broadway musicals delighted theatergoers. Many musicals offered light entertainment, while others addressed the current hardships through songs, such as "Brother, Can You Spare a Dime?"

Your Turn Reread paragraphs 1 and 2 on page 54.

COLLABORATE

- What is the author comparing and contrasting? _____

  _____

  _____

  _____

- What is the central idea of these two paragraphs? _____

  _____

  _____

When you write an expository text, you must have a central idea. You need to support your central idea with relevant evidence, such as facts. Before writing, you should decide which text structure to use to present your evidence. For example, you may use cause and effect, compare and contrast, or problem and solution.

CHECK IN 1 2 3 4

? **How do this photograph and the selections *Bud, Not Buddy* and "Musical Impressions of the Great Depression" demonstrate how sharing music can affect people?**

COLLABORATE

Talk About It Look at the photograph. Read the caption. With a partner, talk about what is going on and how it makes you feel.

Cite Text Evidence Circle details in the photograph that help you understand what people are feeling. **Draw a box** around the main focus of the photo.

Write The photograph and selections show _____

_____

_____

_____

_____

_____

_____

Portrait of Ella Fitzgerald with Dizzy Gillespie, Ray Brown, and other musicians at the Downbeat Club in New York in 1947.

William P. Gottlieb/Ira and Leonore S. Gershwin Fund Collection, Music Division, Library of Congress

CHECK IN ⟩ 1 ⟩ 2 ⟩ 3 ⟩ 4 ⟩

My Goal — I know how sharing experiences helps people change.

Write Song Lyrics

Many characters you read about used music to help them cope during the Great Depression. What qualities do they share that helped them triumph over their hardships and disappointments?

1 Look at your Build Knowledge notes in your reader's notebook.

2 Write song lyrics that describe the qualities the characters have in common that helped them triumph over the hardships and disappointments of the time.

3 Use examples from the texts you read. Use the new vocabulary words you learned.

Think about what you learned in this text set. Fill in the bars on page 37.

Build Knowledge

Build Vocabulary

 Write new words you learned about activities that affect the environment. Draw lines and circles for the words you write.

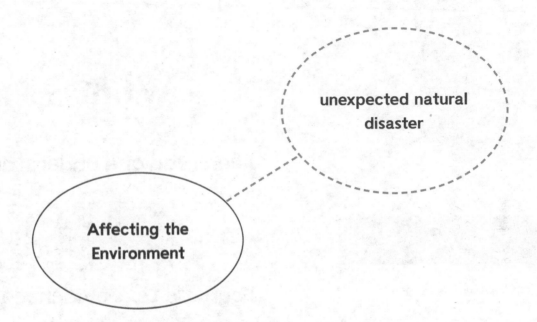

unexpected natural disaster

Affecting the Environment

 Go online to **my.mheducation.com** and read the "Leaving a Trace" Blast. Think about some ways that human activities might continue to affect the natural world. Then blast back your response.

Think about what you already know. Fill in the bars. We all do better with practice.

What I Know Now

I can read and understand argumentative text.

1 2 3 4

I can use text evidence to respond to argumentative text.

1 2 3 4

I know how natural events and human activities affect the environment.

1 2 3 4

Key
1 = I do not understand.
2 = I understand but need more practice.
3 = I understand.
4 = I understand and can teach someone.

STOP You will come back to the next page later.

> Think about what you learned. Fill in the bars. Good job!

What I Learned

I can read and understand argumentative text.

1 > 2 > 3 > 4

I can use text evidence to respond to argumentative text.

1 > 2 > 3 > 4

I know how natural events and human activities affect the environment.

1 > 2 > 3 > 4

TIME for **KiDS**

My Goal I can read and understand argumentative text.

TAKE NOTES

As you read, make note of interesting words and important information.

_____

_____

_____

_____

_____

_____

_____

_____

_____

_____

_____

_____

_____

_____

Kirk Weddle/Photodisc/Getty Images

Essential Question

?

How do natural events and human activities affect the environment?

Read two different views on the arrival of new species into the United States.

It's hard to imagine life without oranges and chickens, which are examples of nonnative species.

Should Plants and Animals from Other Places Live Here?

New Arrivals Welcome

Nonnative species are good for the economy—and they taste good, too!

Some of America's important recent inhabitants are plants and animals. Called *nonnative species*, these creatures arrive here from other regions or countries. Nonnative species are known as *invasive* when they harm the environment, our health, or the economy. Invasive species often take over a **widespread** area and overwhelm native wildlife. The population of some native species has **declined** because of a few newcomers, but the news is not all bad. We would be a lot worse off without some of them.

In Florida, for example, about 2,000 species of familiar plants and animals are nonnative. These include oranges, chickens, and sugarcane. In fact, 90 percent of farm sales can be traced directly to nonnative species.

Nonnative species help to control insects and other pests that harm crops. Some scientists **identify** a pest's natural enemy and bring in nonnative enemy species, such as insects, to kill the pests. Killing the pests is a good thing, and an even better result is that pesticide use is reduced. Vedalia beetles were transported here from Australia to eat insects that killed citrus fruit. The beetles completed their mission without any side effects. They also help keep citrus farmers in business!

Not all new arrivals benefit humans. However, many nonnative species are just what the doctor ordered. Many of the dogs and cats we love so much originated in other parts of the world. Would you want to ban Labrador retrievers and Siamese cats? Creatures like these surely make our lives and our nation better!

ARGUMENTATIVE TEXT

FIND TEXT EVIDENCE

Read

Paragraphs 1–2
Author's Perspective

Write the author's perspective about nonnative species.

_____

_____

Underline the details that support this claim.

Paragraphs 3–4
Ask and Answer Questions

Write a question you can ask to check your understanding about the plan to control insects and pests. Circle the answer.

_____

_____

_____

Reread
Author's Craft

Why does the author talk about both invasive nonnative species and helpful nonnative species?

FIND TEXT EVIDENCE

Read

Paragraphs 1–4

Author's Perspective

Write the author's claim about nonnative species.

_____

_____

Underline specific examples the author gives to support this claim.

Paragraph 5

Root Words

How does the Latin root *clus,* meaning "to shut," help you know what *conclusion* means?

_____

_____

Reread

Author's Craft

Use what you read to make an inference on how people can help prevent the spread of harmful invasive species.

TIME for KiDS

COUNTERPOINT

A Growing Problem

Thousands of foreign plant and animal species threaten our country.

Visitors to the Florida Everglades expect to see alligators, not pythons. These huge snakes are native to Southeast Asia. But about 150,000 of the reptiles are crawling through the Everglades. The **probable** reason they got there is that pet owners dumped the snakes in the wild. Now the nonnative pythons have become a **widespread** menace, threatening to reduce the population of endangered native species.

Some nonnative species may be useful, but others are harmful to the nation. It costs the U.S. more than $120 billion each year to repair the damage these species cause to the environment. The trouble occurs when nonnative species become invasive. Invasive species are a nuisance just about everywhere in the nation. For example, the Asian carp, which was introduced unintentionally to the U.S., has been able to **thrive** in the Mississippi River and now threatens the Great Lakes ecosystem. Because of its large appetite, the population of native fish has gone down.

Some germs are also invasive species, and they are especially harmful to humans. One, the avian influenza virus, came to the U.S. carried by birds. This microbe can cause a serious lung **disorder** in infected people.

Some **agricultural** experts have introduced nonnative species on purpose to improve the environment. However, this can sometimes create **unexpected** problems. A hundred years ago, melaleuca trees were brought to Florida from Australia to stabilize swampy areas. Now millions of the trees blanket the land, crowding out native plants and harming endangered plants and animals.

The facts about this alien invasion lead to one conclusion: We must remove invasive species and keep new ones from our shores.

IrinaMos/Shutterstock

Nonnative Species: Benefits and Costs

Over the years, about 50,000 nonnative species have entered the U.S. These four examples show the positive and negative impacts they can have.

SPECIES	NATIVE LAND	WHEN AND HOW INTRODUCED TO U.S.	POSITIVE IMPACT	NEGATIVE IMPACT
Horse	Europe	Early 1500s, on purpose	Used for work, transportation, and recreation	Made large-scale wars possible
Kudzu	Asia	Early 1800s, on purpose	Stops soil erosion	Crowds out native plants
Olives	Middle East and Europe	Early 1700s, on purpose, cultivation began in 1800s	Major food and cooking oil source, important industry in California	Uses much of the limited supply of water in California
Mediterranean Fruit Fly	Sub-Saharan Africa	1929 (first recorded), accidentally	May be a food source for creatures such as spiders	Destroys 400 species of plants, including citrus and vegetable crops

(t to b) Ingram Publishing; Matt Meadows/Peter Arnold/Getty Images; Emilio Simion/Photodisc/Getty Images; Photo by Jack Dykinga/USDA

This community is trying to control the invasive melaleuca plant that has taken over this marsh.

Summarize

Use your notes to summarize the central ideas of the opposing arguments presented in the selection. Be sure to include the relevant reasons and details that support these arguments.

FIND TEXT EVIDENCE

Read

Charts and Headings

Look at the chart. Which species do you think had more of an impact on people than on the environment? Explain your answer.

_____
_____
_____
_____
_____
_____
_____
_____
_____
_____

Reread

Author's Craft

Why do you think this chart was used to end the selection?

Vocabulary

Use the example sentences to talk with a partner about each word. Then answer the questions.

agricultural

Sam and Gina sell apples and other **agricultural** products at the farmers' market.

How do agricultural products make a difference in your life?

_____

_____

declined

Because many businesses closed, the town had clearly **declined** over the years.

What might happen if a restaurant's profits have declined?

_____

_____

disorder

The veterinarian examined the cow for a stomach **disorder**.

What kind of medical disorder might keep you home from school?

_____

_____

identify

People are able to **identify** my dog by his long ears.

How would you quickly identify your best friend in a crowd?

_____

_____

probable

The **probable** cause of the shattered window was Jack and his soccer ball.

What type of weather is most probable in the winter where you live?

_____

_____

Build Your Word List Pick a word you found interesting in the selection you read. Look up synonyms and antonyms of the word in a print or digital thesaurus, and write them in your reader's notebook.

thrive

Some plants manage to grow and **thrive** even in snow.

What would you do to help a pet thrive?

_____

_____

_____

unexpected

Shoveling the snow was hard work, but it was made easier by the **unexpected** help of our neighbors.

What kind of unexpected event would make you change your plans?

_____

_____

_____

widespread

Starlings, introduced from England, are now a **widespread** bird species.

What is a good example of a widespread fad?

_____

_____

Root Words

A **root word** is the basic word part that gives a word its main meaning. Knowing the meaning of a root is a key to identifying many words that share that root.

🔍 FIND TEXT EVIDENCE

In the first paragraph of "New Arrivals Welcome" on page 65, I read the word invasive. *It has the same root as* invade: vas *and* vad *both come from a Latin word meaning "to go." Something invasive goes into areas beyond its boundaries.*

Nonnative species are known as invasive when they harm the environment, our health, or the economy.

Your Turn Use the roots below to figure out the meanings of words from "New Arrivals Welcome" and "A Growing Problem." List other words you know that contain those roots.

Roots: *nativus* = to be born   *avis* = bird

nonnative, *page 65* _____

avian, *page 66* _____

CHECK IN 1 2 3 4

Matt Meadows/Peter Arnold/Getty Images

Ask and Answer Questions

To check your understanding of an argumentative text, pause at different points and ask yourself questions about what you have read so far. Then look for answers. You can also generate questions about the whole text when you have finished to help deepen your understanding.

 FIND TEXT EVIDENCE

After you read the article "New Arrivals Welcome" on page 65, you might ask yourself, *What is the central idea of this article? What does the author want me to understand about this article?*

Page 65

In Florida, for example, about 2,000 species of familiar plants and animals are nonnative. These include oranges, chickens, and sugarcane. In fact, 90 percent of farm sales can be traced directly to nonnative species.

When I reread, I learn to answer my question. The central idea is that many species in the United States are nonnative but can be very useful to us. Examples such as oranges and sugarcane support this.

COLLABORATE

Your Turn Ask and answer a question about "A Growing Problem" on page 66. Reread the article as necessary. As you reread, use the strategy Ask and Answer Questions. Write your question and answer.

_____

_____

_____

Quick Tip

Some questions you can ask yourself include:

- *Why am I reading this text?*

- *What important details are given?*

- *What am I unclear about?*

- *What connections can I make between information in the article and what I already know?*

CHECK IN 1 2 3 4

Charts and Headings

"New Arrivals Welcome" and "A Growing Problem" are argumentative texts. Argumentative text tries to persuade a reader to support a claim, or argument. The author makes a claim and uses reasons and evidence for or against an argument. Argumentive text may include text features, such as charts and headings.

 FIND TEXT EVIDENCE

Both selections reveal the authors' arguments about nonnative species. Both authors support their arguments with reasons and evidence. A chart has headings and information for comparing the two arguments.

Readers to Writers

When writers write to persuade, they need to give information that is easy to read and understand. Many writers include charts. Charts are a good way to give information in an easy-to-read format. How could you use a chart in your own writing to achieve your purposes?

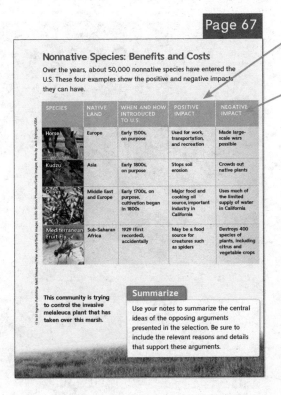

Page 67

Nonnative Species: Benefits and Costs

Over the years, about 50,000 nonnative species have entered the U.S. These four examples show the positive and negative impacts they can have.

SPECIES	NATIVE LAND	WHEN AND HOW INTRODUCED TO U.S.	POSITIVE IMPACT	NEGATIVE IMPACT
Horse	Europe	Early 1500s, on purpose	Used for work, transportation, and recreation	Made large-scale wars possible
Kudzu	Asia	Early 1800s, on purpose	Stops soil erosion	Crowds out native plants
Olives	Middle East and Europe	Early 1700s, on purpose, cultivation began in 1800s	Major food and cooking oil source, important industry in California	Uses much of the limited supply of water in California
Mediterranean Fruit Fly	Sub-Saharan Africa	1929 (first recorded), accidentally	May be a food source for creatures such as spiders	Destroys 400 species of plants, including citrus and vegetable crops

This community is trying to control the invasive melaleuca plant that has taken over this marsh.

Summarize

Use your notes to summarize the central ideas of the opposing arguments presented in the selection. Be sure to include the relevant reasons and details that support these arguments.

Chart
A chart organizes information so it can be analyzed.

Headings
Headings identify the main categories of information.

 COLLABORATE **Your Turn** Analyze the information in the chart on page 67. Identify a species that has a mostly positive impact and one that has a mostly negative impact. Explain your conclusions.

_____

_____

_____

_____

CHECK IN 1 2 3 4

Author's Perspective

In an argumentative text, the **author's perspective** is the author's attitude about a topic. To find an author's perspective, look at the author's reasons and details used to explain the argument for or against an idea. Pay attention to the author's choice of words to help you identify his or her claim.

🔍 FIND TEXT EVIDENCE

I see from the title "A Growing Problem" on page 66 that the author might have a negative perspective toward nonnative species. The word threaten *expresses a negative emotion, and the facts about pythons support a negative perspective.*

Details	Author's Perspective
"A Growing Problem"	The author opposes nonnative species because many become invasive, or hurt native species.
"threaten our country"	
150,000 pythons a "menace"	
Asian carp eat native fish	
"crowding out native plants"	

Your Turn Identify details in "New Arrivals Welcome," and write them in your graphic organizer on page 73. Then identify the author's perspective.

CHECK IN 〉 1 〉 2 〉 3 〉 4 〉

Photo by Jack Dykinga/USDA

72   Unit 5 • Text Set 3

Details	Author's Perspective

Respond to Reading

COLLABORATE

Discuss the prompt below. Use your notes and text evidence to support your answer.

Did you find one author's argument more convincing than the other? Explain your answer.

_____

_____

_____

_____

_____

_____

_____

_____

_____

_____

_____

_____

Quick Tip

Use these sentence starters to discuss the text and to organize text evidence.

- *I found the argument more convincing because . . .*
- *The author points out that . . .*
- *The author gives examples . . .*

Grammar Connections

As you write your response, you can use comparative forms to talk about the two different arguments. When you compare two ideas, use *more, less, better* and *worse*. For more than two ideas, use *most, least, best,* and *worst*.

CHECK IN 1 2 3 4

Environmental Changes

COLLABORATE

When some nonnative species arrive from other places, they may have different effects on their new environment. Choose one nonnative species to create a mock blog report in which you predict its effect on the ecosystem. Work collaboratively in a large group.

Step 1 **Set a Goal** To help you focus your research, create a research plan. Decide what types of information you will include as you answer these questions:

- What animal or plant species will you choose?
- How will you research the species you choose?
- How will you present your mock blog report?
- Do you want to include videos, music, or other recordings? Do you want to include links to other websites?

What additional types of information could you present?

_____

_____

Step 2 **Identify Sources** Discuss how you will gather information from credible print or online sources.

Step 3 **Find and Record Information** Take notes and cite your sources.

Step 4 **Organize and Synthesize Information** Organize your notes. Draft your blog report. Explain why changes in the environment might be harmful.

Step 5 **Create and Present** Complete your blog report. After you finish, present your work to the class.

Starlings are invasive birds that travel in huge flocks. They steal food from other animals as they forage.

In addition to photos, what audio and/or visual might you use in a blog about invasive starlings?

_____

_____

_____

_____

Szczepan Klejbuk/Shutterstock.com

CHECK IN 〉 1 〉 2 〉 3 〉 4

The Case of the Missing Bees

Literature Anthology:
pages 386–389

 Why does the author begin the selection with a question?

 Talk About It Reread the first paragraph on **Literature Anthology** page 387. Talk with a partner about what the question helps you understand about bees.

Cite Text Evidence How does the author organize the first paragraph? Write text evidence in the chart.

Clues

Author's Purpose

 Make Inferences

Reread the question at the beginning of the paragraph. Can you answer it? Is the subject of the question interesting? What inference can you make about why the author includes the question based on your answers?

Write The author begins the article with a question to _____

_____

_____

CHECK IN 1 2 3 4

How does the author's use of headings help you understand his or her perspective about pesticides?

Talk About It Look at the headings on **Literature Anthology** pages 388–389. Turn to a partner and discuss how the headings help the author tell how he or she feels about pesticides.

Cite Text Evidence What words and phrases support the author's headings? Write text evidence, and tell how it shows the author's perspective.

Quick Tip
Headings in a chart identify the main categories of information. As you read, think about how the headings in the article have a similar purpose.

The Unusual Suspects	Are Pesticides to Blame?	Author's Perspective

Write The author uses headings to _____

_____

_____

_____

CHECK IN 1 2 3 4

Respond to Reading

My Goal I can use text evidence to respond to argumentative text.

COLLABORATE Discuss the prompt below. Use your notes and text evidence to support your answer.

Think about how each argumentative article is organized. Which author's style is more convincing? Why?

_____

_____

_____

_____

_____

_____

_____

_____

_____

_____

_____

_____

Quick Tip

Use these sentence starters to talk about and cite text evidence.

- _The author of "A Germ of an Idea" thinks . . ._

- _The author of "Pointing to Pesticides" believes . . ._

- _The way the authors organize information helps me see that . . ._

DanielPrudek/iStock/Getty Images

CHECK IN 1 > 2 > 3 > 4 >

Busy, Beneficial Bees

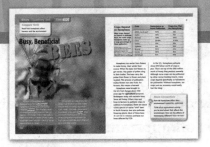

Literature Anthology:
pages 390–391

1   In the U.S., honeybees pollinate about $15 billion worth of crops a year. That's on top of the $150 million worth of honey they produce annually. Although some crops can be pollinated by other nectar-feeding insects, many crops depend specifically on honeybees for pollination. Without honeybees, our crops and our economy would really feel the sting!

Reread paragraph 1. Underline how the author feels about honeybees. Write it here:

_____

_____

_____

Crops Depend on Honeybees

Many crops depend on insects to pollinate them. For some crops, honeybees make up a large percentage of those pollinators.

Crop	Dependence on Insect Pollination	Proportion That Are Honeybees
Alfalfa, hay & seed	100%	60%
Apples	100%	90%
Almonds	100%	100%
Citrus	20–80%	10–90%
Cotton	20%	90%
Soybeans	10%	50%
Broccoli	100%	90%
Carrots	100%	90%
Cantaloupe	80%	90%

Numbers based on estimates in 2000. Source: Compiled by CRS using values reported in R. A. Morse, and N.W. Calderone, *The Value of Honey Bees as Pollinators of U.S. Crops in 2000,* March 2000, Cornell University.

COLLABORATE

Reread the section "Crops Depend on Honeybees." Talk with a partner about why the author includes the chart in this selection. **Circle** text evidence to support your discussion.

Make marks in the table beside the top four crops that depend on insect and honeybee pollination.

? How does the author use a table to help you understand why bees are so important?

Talk About It Reread the table on page 79. With a partner, discuss how it helps support the author's perspective about honeybees.

Cite Text Evidence What information in the table helps support the author's perspective about the importance of bees? Write text evidence in the chart.

Quick Tip

When you read the table, look at the headings for each column first (top row). Then read the information in each row, comparing the second and third columns.

Evidence	Author's Perspective

Write I understand why bees are so important because the author uses a table to _____

_____

_____

_____

Photo by Stephen Ausmus - USDA-ARS

CHECK IN 1 2 3 4

Puns

Puns are examples of figurative language. They are sometimes called "a play on words" because they are words or phrases used in a funny way that suggest a different meaning. Writers may use puns to make a joke, but also to send a message to readers.

FIND TEXT EVIDENCE

In "Busy, Beneficial Bees," the author ends the paragraph about honeybees with a pun.

> Without honeybees, our crops and our economy would really feel the sting!

Your Turn Reread paragraph 1 on page 79.

- What is the central idea of the paragraph? _____

  _____

  _____

- How does the central idea and what you know about bees help you determine the meaning of the pun? _____

  _____

  _____

Readers to Writers

If you want to use puns in your writing, you can find ideas for puns in books or online, or you can write your own. However, choose carefully. Make sure a pun says what you intend it to say and that your readers will understand the play on words.

Try writing a pun.

_____

_____

_____

_____

_____

_____

CHECK IN 1 2 3 4

? How do the speaker in the poem and the authors of "The Case of the Missing Bees" and "Busy, Beneficial Bees" help you understand their perspectives about how humans and animals affect each other?

COLLABORATE

Talk About It Read the poem. Talk with a partner about who the speaker is talking to and what the message is.

Cite Text Evidence **Circle** words and phrases in the poem that tell what the speaker asks children not to do. **Underline** how the speaker says the animals will react to kindness. Think about this perspective and how it compares to the perspectives of the authors of the selections you read this week.

Write I know how the speaker and the authors feel about how humans and animals interact because _____

_____

_____

_____

_____

_____

_____

Kindness to Animals

Little children, never give
Pain to things that feel and live:
Let the gentle robin come
For the crumbs you save at home,—
As his meat you throw along
He'll repay you with a song;
Never hurt the timid hare
Peeping from her green grass lair,
Let her come and sport and play
On the lawn at close of day.

— Anonymous

CHECK IN 1 > 2 > 3 > 4

Write an Editorial

Think about how nonnative species, natural events, and human activities have affected the ecosystems in the texts you read.

1. Look at your Build Knowledge notes in your reader's notebook.

2. Write an editorial in response to the following question: Why should we make habitat conservation a priority?

3. Explain why it is important to prioritize habitat conservation. Then recommend what we can do to conserve these habitats. Support your ideas with examples from the texts. Use the new vocabulary words you learned.

Think about what you learned in this text set. Fill in the bars on page 63.

Think about what you already know. Fill in the bars. Now let's get started!

Key
1 = I do not understand.
2 = I understand but need more practice.
3 = I understand.
4 = I understand and can teach someone.

What I Know Now

I can write a research report.

> 1 > 2 > 3 > 4 >

I can write a personal narrative.

> 1 > 2 > 3 > 4 >

Think about what you learned.
Fill in the bars. The more you write,
the more you'll improve.

What I Learned

I can write a research report.

1 > 2 > 3 > 4

I can write a personal narrative.

1 > 2 > 3 > 4

Expert Model

Features of a Research Report

A research report is an expository text that informs readers about a topic based on relevant information gathered from multiple sources. A research report:

- presents a strong central idea about a topic and is developed with relevant details

- provides an overview of examples, facts, and explanations gathered from research

- uses a logical text structure from beginning to end and includes a strong introduction and conclusion

Literature Anthology:
pages 346–361

Word Wise

On page 347, the author begins the introduction to the topic by using language that is entertaining and easy for readers to understand. This helps readers feel that the author is talking to them about a topic she finds interesting.

Analyze an Expert Model Studying expository texts will help you learn how to plan and write a research report. **Reread** the first paragraph of *When Is a Planet Not a Planet?* on page 347 in the **Literature Anthology**. Write your answers to the questions below.

How does the author spark your interest in the topic? Use text evidence.

_____

_____

What specific detail about Mercury and Pluto does the author give?

_____

_____

Plan: Choose Your Topic

Brainstorm With a partner, brainstorm a list of scientific advancements made in the twenty-first century. Scientific advancements can include new knowledge and understanding, as well as new inventions. Write your ideas below.

Quick Tip

If you are unsure which scientific advancements were made in the twenty-first century, you can ask your teacher for assistance.

To help you choose your topic, think about what you are most interested in. What do you want to learn about this topic?

_____

_____

_____

_____

Writing Prompt Choose one scientific advancement of the twenty-first century from your list. Write a research report telling about this advancement. Include why the advancement is important.

I will write about _____

Purpose and Audience Think about who will read or hear your report. Will your **purpose** be to inform, persuade, or entertain?

My purpose for writing is to _____.

Plan In your writer's notebook, make a central idea and relevant details chart to plan your writing. Fill in the central idea with the scientific advancement you have chosen. Fill in the details as you research your topic.

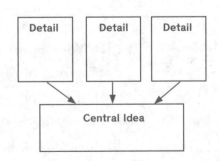

Plan: Relevant Evidence

Choose Relevant Evidence From Sources After you find reliable resources for your report, choose the evidence that is most relevant, or relates to your topic. Use the central idea for your topic to help you focus on the information you need. As you read your sources, think about these questions:

- Have I read the source carefully and critically?

- Is this information good evidence for one of my main points?

- Have I used a variety of sources in order to find different kinds of information? Other sources may include additional information.

List two pieces of relevant evidence for your report.

1 _____

_____

2 _____

_____

Cite Your Sources Note the source of each piece of relevant evidence you find, including page number or website. Avoid plagiarism. Even if you plan to paraphrase information in your own words, it is important to cite the sources you used in your bibliography. Use quotes exactly the way they appear in the source.

CHECK IN 1 2 3 4

Draft

Elaboration Authors use elaboration to support and develop their central ideas. Elaboration includes convincing facts, quotations, or examples about the topic. In the example below from "Changing Views of Earth," the author gives facts, such as a time period, and examples, such as "five kilometers," about the height that airplanes could lift scientists.

> Kites and balloons were hard to control. . . . The development of aircraft in the early 1900s promised safer ways to observe Earth's surface and the atmosphere above it. . . . airplanes lifted scientists to a height of five kilometers and more.

Now use the paragraph as a model to write about the twenty-first-century scientific advancement you chose for your topic. State your central idea. Then provide elaborative details from your research that are relevant to your central idea.

_____

_____

_____

_____

_____

Grammar Connections

Make sure that any pronoun you use relates to the noun, or antecedent, that comes before it. In the excerpt, the pronoun *it* refers to the Earth's surface.

Write a Draft Use your central idea and details chart to help you write your draft in your writer's notebook. Don't forget to write an introduction that sparks interest in your topic. Remember to indent each paragraph.

CHECK IN 1 2 3 4

Revise

Sentence Structure Effective writers make sure that their sentence structure clearly communicates their ideas. Sometimes combining ideas can make your sentences clearer. You can also improve the sentence structure by rearranging, or moving, ideas in the sentence.

Here is an example: *Sally knows the dog is big, she knows the dog is brown, and the dog lives next door*. These phrases all describe things Sally knows about the same dog, so they can be combined. *Sally knows the dog next door is big and brown*. This makes it clear that the writer is talking about the same dog that lives next door.

Read the sentence below. How might you revise it to combine ideas?

> NASA launched dozens of satellites, and these
> satellites peered deep into endless space.

_____

_____

_____

 Revision Revise your draft. Think about what is the most logical structure to present your information about the history and importance of your scientific advancement. Remember to use transitional words and phrases to connect your ideas.

Word Wise

When you revise, check that sentences are clear and the ideas are easy to follow. You may need to rearrange ideas. For example, *She saw stars looking out the window*. This sentence structure makes it seem like the stars are looking out the window. *Looking out the window, she saw stars* makes more sense.

CHECK IN   1   2   3   4

wavebreakmedia/Shutterstock.com

Peer Conferences

Review a Draft Listen carefully as a partner reads his or her draft aloud. Tell what you like about the draft. Use these sentence starters to help you discuss your partner's draft.

I enjoyed this part of your draft because . . .
That detail does not seem relevant. Can you explain why . . .
I am not sure about the order of . . .

Partner Feedback After you take turns giving each other feedback, write one of the suggestions from your partner that you will use in your revision.

_____

_____

Revision After you finish your peer conference, use the Revising Checklist to help you make your research report better. Remember to use the full expository rubric on pages 220–223 to help you with your revision.

Digital Tools

For more information about how to have peer conferences watch "Peer Conferencing." Go to **my.mheducation.com**.

Revising Checklist

- ☐ Does my writing fit my purpose and audience?
- ☐ Did I include enough evidence from multiple sources? Did I cite my sources correctly?
- ☐ Did I include relevant details that support the central idea?
- ☐ Are my facts and details presented in a logical structure, or order? Did I include a strong introduction and conclusion?

Edit and Proofread

When you **edit** and **proofread** your writing, you look for and correct mistakes in spelling, punctuation, capitalization, and grammar. Reading through a revised draft multiple times can help you make sure you're correcting any errors. Use the checklist below to edit your sentences.

✓ Editing Checklist

- ☐ Do all sentences begin with a capital letter and end with a punctuation mark?
- ☐ Are there any run-on sentences or sentence fragments?
- ☐ Do all sentences have subject-verb agreement?
- ☐ Are clauses, appositives, and quotes punctuated correctly?
- ☐ Are proper nouns and abbreviations, initials, and acronyms capitalized correctly?
- ☐ Are referenced titles italicized or underlined?
- ☐ Are all words spelled correctly?

Tech Tip

Spellcheckers are useful tools in word-processing programs, but they may not recognize incorrect words. For example, if you meant to use *we'll* but typed *well* instead, the spellchecker might not catch it. That is why it's important to also do a careful reading.

Grammar Connections

When you proofread your report, make sure that you have capitalized proper nouns, such as names, places, organizations, and events, if they have a specific title or name.

List two mistakes you found as you proofread your research report.

1 _____

_____

2 _____

_____

Publish, Present, and Evaluate

Publishing When you publish your writing, you create a neat final copy that is free of mistakes. If you are not using a computer, write legibly in print or cursive.

Presentation When you are ready to present your work, rehearse your presentation. Use the Presenting Checklist to help you.

Evaluate After you publish, use the full expository rubric on pages 220–223 to evaluate it.

What did you do successfully? _____

_____

What needs more work? _____

_____

Turn to page 85. Fill in the bars to show what you learned.

✓ **Presenting Checklist**

☐ Look at the audience.

☐ Speak slowly, clearly, and loudly.

☐ Display any visuals so that everyone can see them.

☐ Answer questions thoughtfully.

My Score			
Purpose, Focus, & Organization (4 pts)	Evidence & Elaboration (4 pts)	Conventions (2 pts)	Total (10 pts)

Expert Model

Features of a Personal Narrative

A personal narrative is a piece of nonfiction writing that tells a story from the author's life. A personal narrative

- is told from the first-person point of view and expresses the writer's thoughts and feelings about a real experience

- uses descriptive and sensory details to help readers understand and visualize the experience

- follows a logical sequence of events from beginning to end, including a satisfying introduction and conclusion

- uses a variety of transitional strategies to connect events

Literature Anthology:
pages 28–31

Word Wise

In the first paragraph on page 29, Roosevelt says, "We drove to the pretty, smiling valley . . ." Authors sometimes use human behaviors to describe nonhuman things. This is called personification. Personification is a type of figurative language. It gives human qualities to an animal or object to help create an image in the reader's mind.

Analyze an Expert Model Studying a personal narrative will help you learn how to write a personal narrative of your own. **Reread** page 29, a segment of Theodore Roosevelt's autobiography, in the **Literature Anthology**. Write your answers to the questions below.

What details from the text tell you that this section of "A Walk with Teddy" is a personal narrative? _____

_____

Look at the first paragraph on page 29. List one example of words or phrases the author uses to show the sequence of events. _____

_____

Plan: Choose Your Topic

Freewrite Think about an event in your life that had a positive impact on the environment. It should be an event that you can remember clearly. These might be events such as planting a class garden, cleaning up a park, or making a bird feeder. Quickly write your ideas without stopping. Then discuss your ideas with a partner.

_____

_____

_____

Writing Prompt Choose one of your ideas that you want to expand into a personal narrative.

I will write my personal narrative about _____

Purpose and Audience Think about who will read or hear your narrative. Will your purpose be to persuade, inform, or entertain them? Then think about the language you will use to write your narrative.

My purpose is to _____

My audience will be _____

I will use _____ language when I write my personal narrative.

Plan Think about what you want your readers to learn about the experience. Ask yourself questions, and answer them in your writer's notebook. Questions to ask might include the following: *Why was the experience important? What did I learn from it? How do I feel about it?* Include specific details in your answers.

Quick Tip

A personal narrative does not need to use the type of formal language you would use in an expository essay. You can use the type of informal language, or tone, you would use when writing a letter or e-mail to a friend.

Plan: Sequence of Events

Sequence of Events Once you have decided on your topic, you will need to plan the sequence, or order, of events in your personal narrative. Following a logical sequence will help readers understand what happened and why. To make sure you cover everything, answer these questions:

- Am I telling the events in the order that makes the most logical sense?

- How, when, and where does my narrative begin?

- Why is this event important? How do I feel as this event is happening?

- Have I used transitional words such as *first, earlier, then, next, after, before, later, meanwhile,* and *last* to show the sequence from beginning to end and signal how events are connected?

List two events you will tell about in the sequence of your narrative.

1 _____

_____

2 _____

_____

Graphic Organizer In your writer's notebook, make a sequence of events graphic organizer to plan your writing. Fill in the boxes with the most important events of your personal narrative in order. Include relevant details. Remember that a personal narrative is told from your first-person point of view and uses words such as *I, me,* and *my.*

> **Quick Tip**
>
> Think about the order in which things happened to you. Write or draw what happened first, next, and so on. Use these sentence starters to help you.
>
> *The story's introduction will include . . .*
>
> *Then I will tell about . . .*
>
> *I will end by . . .*

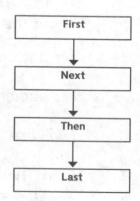

First

↓

Next

↓

Then

↓

Last

CHECK IN 1 〉 2 〉 3 〉 4

Draft

Description Writers of personal narratives use vivid descriptive and sensory language to tell about events. They use words and phrases that allow readers to visualize the experience and understand the writer's thoughts and feelings about it. In the sentence below from "A Life in the Woods," Thoreau describes what he sees and feels.

> At length he uttered one of those prolonged howls, as if calling on the god of the loons to aid him, and immediately there came a wind from the east and rippled the surface, and filled the whole air with misty rain, and I was impressed.

Now use the above excerpt as a model to write a paragraph that could be a part of your personal narrative. Think carefully about your descriptions.

_____

_____

_____

_____

_____

Word Wise

To help you come up with descriptive and sensory words, close your eyes and think about the experience you are describing. Use words that describe what you saw, heard, smelled, tasted, and felt. You can also use a thesaurus to help you find an appropriate descriptive word.

Write a Draft Use your sequence of events graphic organizer to help you write your draft in your writer's notebook. As you write your draft, use transitional words and phrases to connect events. Include plenty of descriptive and sensory details to help them understand your experience. Finally, remember to indent each paragraph.

CHECK IN 1 > 2 > 3 > 4

Revise

Strong Conclusions An effective personal narrative has a strong conclusion that gives a sense of closure, or ending. A strong conclusion also describes how the narrative is resolved. Combining ideas may make a conclusion stronger by helping readers focus on the experiences that are most important to the writer. Read the paragraph below. Then revise the last four sentences to make a stronger conclusion.

> Last fall, I decided to join my school's Saving the Environment Club. Everyone joining the club had to research a topic and present a slideshow. I was afraid that I would forget the words to my presentation, so I practiced every night. Finally, it was time for my presentation. I stood in the front of the room and looked out at the other kids' faces. Everyone looked so friendly! I wasn't nervous anymore. I presented my slideshow, and then I heard clapping. I had a good presentation and I was good at it. I smiled. I was happy.

_____

_____

_____

Word Wise

When you use signal words in your conclusion, make sure to keep the sequence of events in mind. Your ideas should be coherent, or easy to follow. _Finally, it was time for my presentation_ is more coherent than _After a while, it was time for my presentation, at last._ Combining the ideas of "after a while" and "at last" by using "finally" makes the sentence easier to understand.

Revision Revise your draft, and check that your conclusion is strong. Does your conclusion tell what happens at the end? Does it show why the experience was important to you?

CHECK IN 1 2 3 4

Peer Conferences

Review a Draft Listen carefully as a partner reads his or her draft aloud. Tell what you like about the draft. Use these sentence starters to help you discuss your partner's draft.

I enjoyed this part of your draft because . . .
You might improve this description by . . .
I have a question about . . .

Partner Feedback After you take turns giving each other feedback, write one of the suggestions from your partner that you will use in your revision.

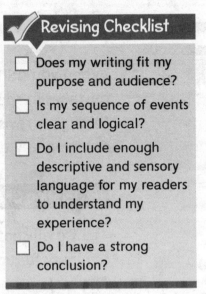

Revising Checklist

- [ ] Does my writing fit my purpose and audience?
- [ ] Is my sequence of events clear and logical?
- [ ] Do I include enough descriptive and sensory language for my readers to understand my experience?
- [ ] Do I have a strong conclusion?

_____

_____

Revision After you finish your peer conference, use the Revising Checklist to help you make your narrative better. Remember to use the full narrative rubric on pages 224–227 to help you with your revision.

Edit and Proofread

When you **edit** and **proofread** your writing, you look for and correct mistakes in spelling, punctuation, capitalization, and grammar. Reading through a revised draft multiple times can help you make sure you're catching any errors. Use the checklist below to edit your narrative.

✓ Editing Checklist

☐ Do all sentences begin with a capital letter and end with a punctuation mark?

☐ Have I used commas correctly?

☐ Do all of my sentences express a complete thought?

☐ Are proper nouns capitalized?

☐ Are quotation marks used correctly?

☐ Are all words spelled correctly?

Grammar Connections

Personal narratives may include dialogue. Lines of dialogue are set off by quotation marks. Make sure you have used quotation marks correctly in any dialogue you write. Use a comma to separate a phrase, such as *she said*, from the quotation itself. For example: *My sister said, "I think that is a terrific idea!"*

List two mistakes you found as you proofread your narrative.

1 _____

_____

2 _____

_____

Publish, Present, and Evaluate

Publishing When you publish your writing, you create a neat final copy that is free of mistakes. If you are not using a computer, write legibly in print or cursive.

Presentation When you are ready to present your work, rehearse your presentation. Use the Presenting Checklist.

Evaluate After you publish, use the full narrative rubric on pages 224–227 to evaluate it.

What did you do successfully? _____

_____

What needs more work? _____

_____

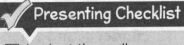

Presenting Checklist

☐ Look at the audience and make eye contact.

☐ Speak clearly, enunciating each word.

☐ Speak loud enough so that everyone can hear you.

☐ Use natural gestures when telling your narrative.

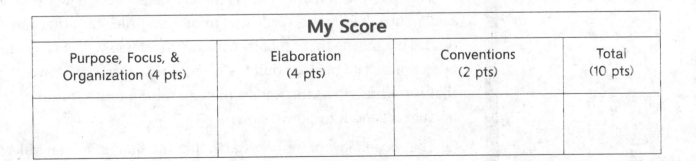

Turn to page 85. Fill in the bars to show what you learned.

My Score			
Purpose, Focus, & Organization (4 pts)	Elaboration (4 pts)	Conventions (2 pts)	Total (10 pts)

My Goal I can read and understand science texts.

TAKE NOTES

Take notes and annotate as you read the passages "Sir Isaac Newton" and "Gravity."

Look for the answer to the question: *How has our understanding of motion and forces changed over time?*

_____

_____

_____

_____

_____

_____

_____

_____

_____

_____

_____

PASSAGE 1 **EXPOSITORY TEXT**

Sir Isaac Newton

Sir Isaac Newton studied physics and math in the 1600s. The laws of motion are among his most famous achievements. But he did not just discover them on his own. Newton learned from other scientists before him who also studied motion, astronomy, and math, such as Galileo and Aristotle. He started with their theories and built on them. He was able to prove some of their theories. He helped our understanding of these concepts to change.

The first law of motion states that an object at rest will stay at rest and an object in motion will stay in motion unless another force acts on it. This means that an object sitting on a table will stay sitting on the table unless you push or pull the object and cause it to move. A ball that is rolling across the floor will keep rolling unless another force like friction acts on it to slow it down.

The second law of motion states that the more mass an object has, the more force it will take to change its acceleration. It will take more force to move a large truck than it will to move a small wagon.

The third law of motion states that for every action there is an equal and opposite reaction. Forces act in pairs. When you push on a box, the box pushes back against you with an opposing, balanced force.

Pixtal/age fotostock

Other scientists since Newton, including Albert Einstein and many others, have continued to build on his ideas. For example, they form new theories to describe the motion of very small objects like electrons or objects that are moving very fast near the speed of light. Our understanding of these concepts may change as new scientists study and test these concepts and form new ideas.

TAKE NOTES

PASSAGE **2** EXPOSITORY TEXT

GRAVITY

When you jump as high as you can, what pulls you back down so you do not float up into space? Gravity is the force that pulls everything to Earth!

Our understanding of gravity has changed over time. Galileo conducted experiments with gravity by dropping objects from a height to see what happened. But Sir Isaac Newton was the first person to realize that there must be a force that pulls the objects to Earth. He concluded that gravity is an attraction between two objects that have mass. Hundreds of years later, Albert Einstein added to Newton's discoveries when he developed new ideas about gravity to explain aspects of light and time.

The pull of gravity increases when an object has more mass. You have gravity. But Earth has a much stronger gravitational pull because it has much more mass than you do! The pull of Earth's gravity is what gives you weight.

gradyreese/iStock/Getty Images

TAKE NOTES

_____
_____
_____
_____
_____
_____
_____
_____
_____
_____
_____
_____
_____
_____
_____
_____
_____
_____
_____
_____
_____
_____

Planets and other objects in our solar system each have a different mass, so they each exert a different amount of gravitational pull on objects. The Moon and Mars have much less mass than Earth, so you would weigh much less there. Jupiter has much more mass than Earth, so you would weigh about two and a half times more on Jupiter!

Did you think that astronauts can float in space because there is no gravity there? The astronauts and their spacecraft still fall toward Earth due to gravity. But because the spacecraft moves so fast, the curve of its fall matches the curve of Earth. This keeps the spacecraft in orbit around Earth instead of hitting Earth's surface.

Newton's principle of gravity keeps all the planets in orbit around the Sun and the Moon in orbit around Earth. No matter where you go in our solar system, you cannot escape gravity!

NASA/Roscosmos

COMPARE THE PASSAGES

Review your notes from "Sir Isaac Newton" and "Gravity." Then use your notes and the Venn diagram below to record how what you learned in the passages is alike and different.

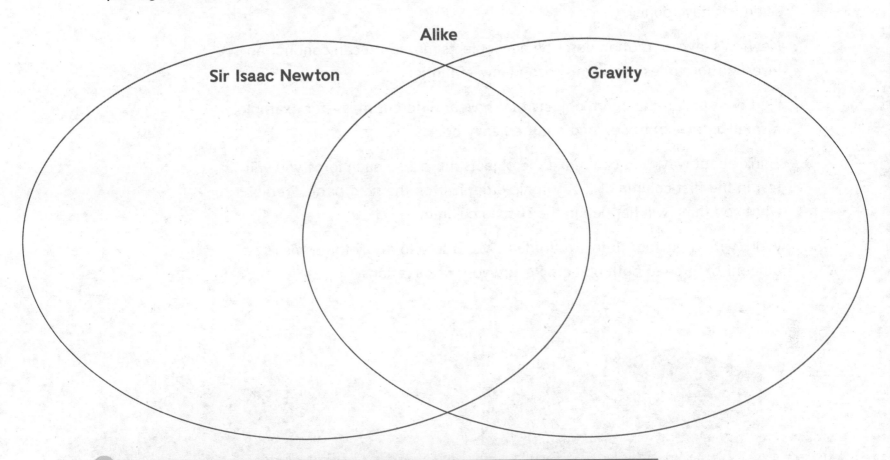

Alike

Sir Isaac Newton

Gravity

Synthesize Information

Think about what you learned about planets in *When Is a Planet Not a Planet?* How does the information in "Sir Isaac Newton" and "Gravity" relate to what you learned about planets? Write your ideas in your reader's notebook.

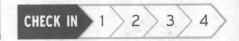

CONNECT TO CONTENT

INVESTIGATE NEWTON'S LAWS

Scientists conduct investigations to test the theories and findings of other scientists. They can repeat the same tests or apply the ideas to new situations. Their observations can support or disprove the work other scientists have done.

Newton's laws of motion describe how objects move. You can conduct an investigation to test Newton's second law of motion.

Find two similar classroom objects that have a different mass—for example, a small lightweight book and a large heavy book.

Think about ways you can make the objects move. List each force you will test in the first column of the graphic organizer on the next page. Predict what you think will happen in the second column.

Work with a partner to test your ideas. Make sure to apply the same amount of force to both objects. Record your observations.

(b) donatas1205/123RF.com; (bl) Christian Delbert/Shutterstock;
(br) Ken Cavanagh/McGraw-Hill Education

RECORD YOUR DATA

Complete the graphic organizer to record your tests, predictions, and observations.

Force	Predictions	Observations

Did your results support Newton's second law of motion? Why or why not?

_____

_____

_____

_____

_____

_____

_____

My Goal I can read and understand social studies texts.

TAKE NOTES

Take notes and annotate as you read the passages "Wind in the Great Plains" and "Dusting Off with Humor."

Look for the answer to the question: *How did changes in the environment affect the people who lived in the Dust Bowl region?*

_____

_____

_____

_____

_____

_____

_____

_____

_____

PASSAGE 1

EXPOSITORY TEXT

WIND IN THE GREAT PLAINS

The wind often plays a role in stories about the Great Plains. Long ago, the North American region was covered with prairie grass and bison. Native Americans who hunted the bison often spoke of wind in their stories. More recent lore includes the story of Dorothy, a girl from Kansas who gets carried by a tornado to a magical land called Oz.

Tornados are so common in the Great Plains that it is nicknamed Tornado Alley. Winds from tornados cause destruction throughout the area. Winds also caused destruction during the Dust Bowl of the 1930s.

After the Civil War, Congress passed several acts encouraging settlers to move to the Great Plains. Weather there could be harsh, but many people took the risk so they could own land and farm it.

Farmers began plowing up many acres of grassland to plant wheat. After World War I, wheat prices fell, forcing farmers to plow up even more land to make a living. They often overplowed the land, causing the soil to become too fine. If it rained regularly, fine soil was not a problem. During a series of serious droughts in the 1930s, the soil began to dry up and blow around.

Then the wind blew dust

Dust Bowl region
Most of the Great Plains region
Tornado Alley

across the plains, burying crops, houses, barns, and buildings. In 1935, Caroline Henderson, living on a farm in Oklahoma, wrote in a letter to a friend, ". . . we have been trying to rescue our home from the accumulations of wind-blown dust which penetrate wherever air can go. It is an almost hopeless task, for there is rarely a day when at some time the dust clouds do not roll over." The Dust Bowl lasted almost a decade. People lost their farms. Some people even left to find work elsewhere.

PASSAGE 2 INFORMATIONAL TEXT

DUSTING OFF with HUMOR

The 1930s Dust Bowl featured huge dust storms that destroyed large areas of the Great Plains. The dust was often thick, and black blizzards of dirt engulfed the ground and air.

During this difficult time, many people in the midwestern states kept a sense of humor. Sharing humorous tall tales and jokes was one way to defeat the ever-present dust storms. For example, a social worker reported that tall tales and jokes brought strength to many people she visited in their Kansas county. In a 1936 article in *The Survey*, she stated that these tales "enlivened," or brightened, people's moods. Below are some examples and explanations of tall tales and jokes from the Dust Bowl era.

The dust was so thick, prairie dogs had to burrow 10 feet in the air! In the southern and central plains, the topsoil had been worn out by farmers and dried to bits by hot, dry, and windy conditions.

TAKE NOTES

_____

_____

_____

_____

_____

_____

_____

_____

_____

_____

_____

_____

_____

_____

_____

_____

_____

_____

TAKE NOTES

_____

_____

_____

_____

_____

_____

_____

_____

_____

_____

_____

_____

_____

_____

_____

_____

_____

_____

_____

_____

He'll be along soon. I just saw his farm go by! During the 1930s, dust blew so far that in May 1934, dust made the US Capitol and the Statue of Liberty, on the East Coast, hard to see. Millions of people lost their land and money.

Did you hear about the farmer who went to the bank for a loan, only to see his land blow past the window? About 2.5 million people moved from the states most affected. It was the largest migration in US history. People moved from Colorado, Kansas, Nebraska, New Mexico, Oklahoma, and Texas. Thousands went to California to start new lives.

Dust storms made planting easy. Farmers threw seeds in the air as the fields went by. Today, we marvel at photos of the storms and the size of the area affected, but perhaps nothing is more amazing than reading these old jokes. After the storms died down, these tall tales and jokes were a testament to the resilience of the people of the Dust Bowl.

COMPARE THE PASSAGES

Use your notes to answer the question on page 108. Record the information needed to compare the two passages.

Wind in the Great Plains	Dusting Off with Humor
Central Idea You Learned	**Central Idea You Learned**

Synthesize Information

Think about what you learned about the 1930s in "The Day the Rollets Got Their Moxie Back" and *Bud, Not Buddy*. How does the information in "Wind in the Great Plains" and "Dusting Off with Humor" help you relate to what you learned in these works of historical fiction? Write your ideas in your reader's notebook.

CHECK IN 》1 》2 》3 》4 》

SOCIAL STUDIES

WRITE A 1-2-3 REPORT ON ENVIRONMENT

> **WIND** In the western states of the Great Plains, a warm, dry wind called the chinook blows down from the Rocky Mountains in winter. Throughout the region, wind is almost constant.
>
> **PLANTS** The main type of plant that grows throughout the Great Plains is grass. Along rivers and in the mountains, there are forests.
>
> **RAIN** The main source of rainfall for the Great Plains is the Gulf of Mexico. The average annual rainfall varies widely throughout the region.

1. **Focus your topic.** Choose one of the subjects in the box above.

2. **Conduct research.** For each subject, two facts are provided. Find three more facts on the subject you have chosen. Make sure to use reliable sources when you look for facts. Remember to cite the sources you used.

3. **Synthesize the details.** In your reader's notebook, write a paragraph that relates your fact collection to the Dust Bowl. Share your work with the class.

Dorothea Lange/Library of Congress

Reflect on Your Learning

COLLABORATE

Talk About It Reflect on what you learned in this unit. Then talk with a partner about how you did.

I am really proud of how I can _____

_____

_____

_____

_____

Something I need to work more on is _____

_____

_____

_____

_____

Share a goal you have with a partner.

My Goal Set a goal for Unit 6. In your reader's notebook, write about what you can do to get there.

Build Knowledge

Essential Question

How do different groups contribute to a cause?

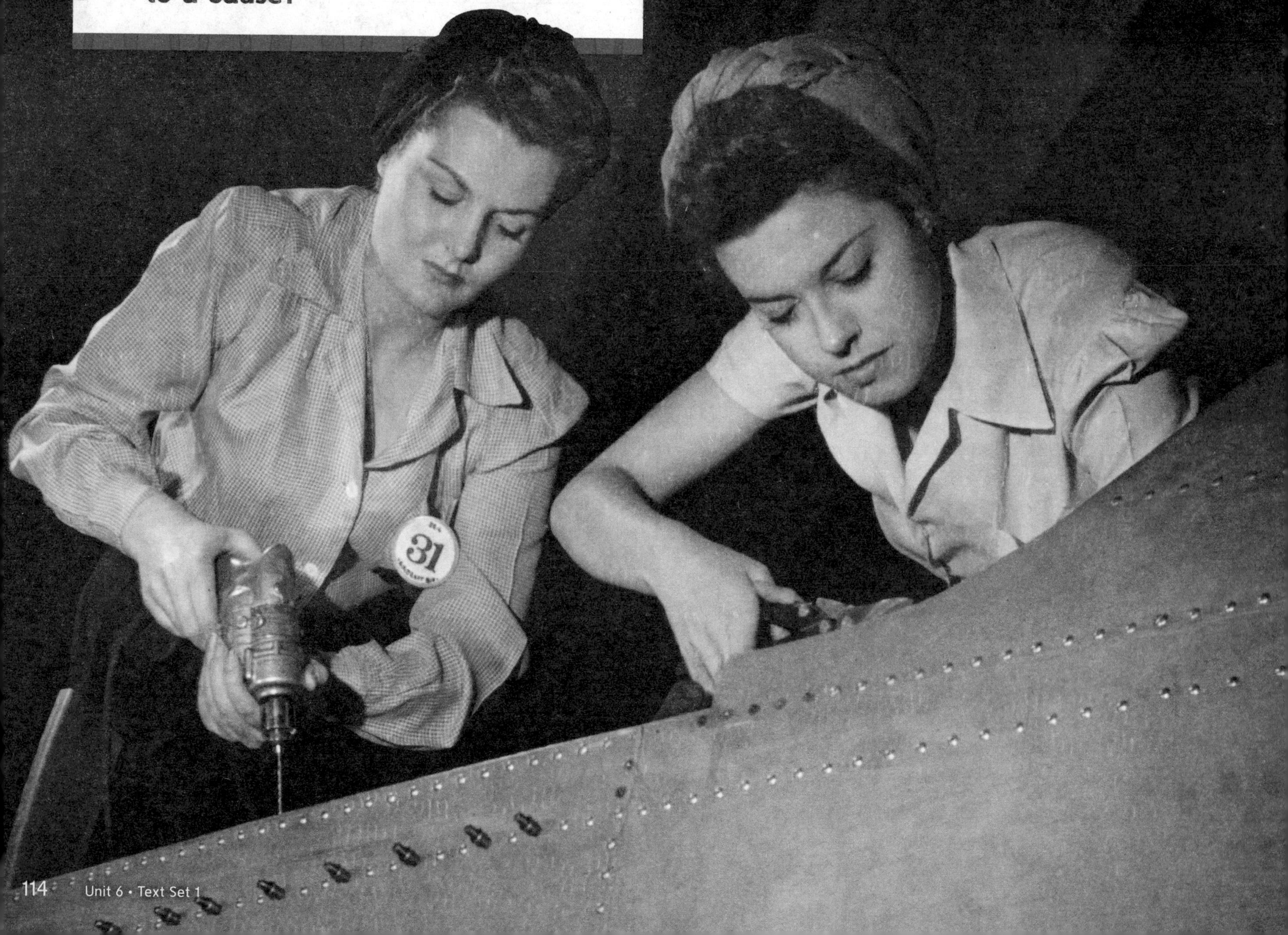

Build Vocabulary

Write new words you learned about the contributions people can make to help a cause. Draw lines and circles for the words you write.

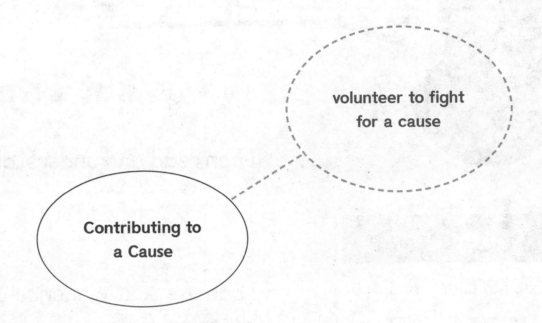

Contributing to a Cause

volunteer to fight for a cause

Go online to **my.mheducation.com** and read the "Outstanding Contributions" Blast. Think about what makes a contribution outstanding and why. Why is it sometimes important to make a contribution? Then blast back your response.

Think about what you already know. Fill in the bars. You'll learn more with practice.

What I Know Now

Key
1 = I do not understand.
2 = I understand but need more practice.
3 = I understand.
4 = I understand and can teach someone.

I can read and understand historical fiction.

1 > 2 > 3 > 4

I can use text evidence to respond to historical fiction.

1 > 2 > 3 > 4

I know how different groups can contribute to a cause.

1 > 2 > 3 > 4

STOP You will come back to the next page later.

Think about what you learned. Fill in the bars. What is getting easier for you?

What I Learned

I can read and understand historical fiction.

1 2 3 4

I can use text evidence to respond to historical fiction.

1 2 3 4

I know how different groups can contribute to a cause.

1 2 3 4

My Goal I can read and understand historical fiction.

TAKE NOTES

As you read, make note of interesting words and important events.

_____

_____

_____

_____

_____

_____

_____

_____

_____

_____

_____

_____

_____

SHIPPED OUT

 Essential Question

How do different groups contribute to a cause?

Read about how a young girl learns how to contribute to the war effort during World War II.

My name is Libby Kendall, and I am a prisoner of war. Well, not really, but some days it feels that way. Just like my dad, I've packed up my things and shipped out. Unlike my dad, however, nothing I do will ever help the Allies win World War II.

My father is a mechanic on a battleship in the Pacific Ocean. I'm trapped in a little apartment above my Aunt Lucia's bakery downtown. Mom says it's just for a few months while she works double shifts at the clothing factory. She makes uniforms, mostly sewing pockets on jackets. I asked her once if she snuck things into the pockets for soldiers to find, like little poems written in calligraphy. She said soldiers wore jackets with pockets to hold tools they might need for war **survival,** not silly things like poetry.

It seems no one appreciates my creative **contributions** to the war effort, but Aunt Lucia says my help to her is important, since both her workers joined the army.

On my first day with Aunt Lucia, she explained the daily **operations** of the bakery. First, we get up before dawn to knead the dough. Next, we bake breads and muffins. Then, while I help customers, Lucia makes cakes and cookies for sale in the afternoon. Whenever the phone rings, she races from the back room to **intercept** the call. She's always worried that it might be bad news, so she wants to be the first to hear it.

After dinner, Aunt Lucia invites neighbors over to listen to the radio. Some are immigrants from a wide **diversity** of backgrounds. Lucia and others help translate the news into several languages for everyone to understand. I always listen closely for any **bulletin** about fighting in the Pacific.

FIND TEXT EVIDENCE

Read

Paragraphs 1–2

Theme

What information supports the idea that different people can contribute to a cause? **Underline** the text evidence. Write your answer here.

_____

_____

_____

_____

Paragraphs 3–5

Summarize

Circle the important details that describe Libby's work. Summarize it.

_____

_____

Reread

Author's Craft

This story uses a first-person point of view. How does that affect the mood of the story?

FIND TEXT EVIDENCE

Read

Paragraphs 1–3
Plot: Flashback

Circle clues that show Libby is thinking about an earlier time.

Paragraph 3
Theme

Underline text evidence that shows the change in Libby's behavior after she learns her dad is joining the navy.

Paragraph 4
Summarize

Summarize how Libby responds to her feelings.

_____

_____

_____

Reread

Author's Craft

Why did the author include the flashback in this story?

I remember how intently my parents read reports about the war, which I rarely understood. They often whispered to one another, and I'd shout out something like, "Speak up! I can't hear you!" They'd frown and leave me alone to talk in private.

One night, they came into the living room and turned off the radio. At first I was angry, but they had serious expressions on their faces. "Our country's at war," Dad said. "The military will be looking for new **recruits**. I know something about boats and ship engines, so I intend to join the navy."

My face grew hot, but my hands felt cold. "You can't just leave," I said. I stomped on the floor for emphasis and stormed off to my bedroom. Looking back on that now, I feel ashamed of how selfishly I had acted.

This morning, Aunt Lucia can tell I'm feeling down. She asks me to help her decorate cupcakes for a fund-raiser tonight. At first I'm not interested. I just slather on frosting and plop a berry on top. Then I realize that I can make red stripes out of strawberries and a patch of blue from blueberries. Soon I have a whole tray of cupcakes decorated like flags to show Aunt Lucia.

"These are wonderful!" Lucia says. "I'm sure they'll sell better than anything else!"

For the first time in weeks, I feel like I've done something right. I think of all the money we might make at the sale, and how it may buy supplies for my father.

"I **enlisted** in the navy to help restore democracy in the world," my dad said on the day he left. "Now you be a good navy daughter and sail straight, young lady."

I promised I would. As he went out the door, I slipped a little poem into his coat pocket. "Here's a little rhyme to pass the day," it said. "I love you back in the U.S.A.!"

I look at the cupcakes and wish I could send one to my dad. Instead, I'll draw a platter on which they're piled high and send the picture off to the Pacific with a letter. That way, my dad will have plenty to share with everyone there.

Summarize

Use your notes to summarize the theme of the story. Be sure to include details about the plot elements, including events and setting.

FIND TEXT EVIDENCE

Read

Paragraphs 1–2

Theme

How does Aunt Lucia try to cheer up Libby? What effect does this have?

_____

_____

_____

Paragraphs 2–5

Homophones

Underline context clues that help you distinguish the meanings of *sale* and *sail*. Write their meanings.

_____

_____

Reread

Author's Craft

What message does the author give readers through Libby's actions?

Vocabulary

Use the example sentences to talk with a partner about each word. Then answer the questions.

bulletin

Kip posted a **bulletin** in the neighborhood about his missing dog.

Why else might you post a bulletin?

_____

_____

contributions

The art exhibit at school will feature **contributions** by many student artists.

What other events depend on contributions from others?

_____

_____

diversity

There was a great **diversity** of breeds at the dog show.

Where else might you see a large diversity of animals?

_____

_____

enlisted

Citizens who have **enlisted** in the military are sworn in before training begins.

Why might people enlist in the military?

_____

_____

intercept

I jumped up to **intercept** the pass and to prevent a touchdown by the other team.

In what other sports might you intercept a ball?

_____

Build Your Word List Pick a word you found interesting in the selection you read. Look up synonyms and antonyms of the word in a thesaurus and write them in your reader's notebook.

operations

The crew began **operations** to clean up after the disaster.

What other operations might help after a disaster?

_____

_____

_____

recruits

The official addressed the new **recruits**.

What kinds of organizations look for new recruits?

_____

_____

_____

survival

Food and water are important for **survival** during an emergency.

What other items are important for survival during an emergency?

_____

_____

Homophones

Sometimes when you read, you come across **homophones**, or words that sound the same, but are spelled differently and have different meanings. Surrounding words and sentences can help you figure out the meaning of a homophone.

🔍 FIND TEXT EVIDENCE

In "Shipped Out" on page 119, I see the words war and wore, which are pronounced the same way. From the surrounding words, I can tell that war means "a large conflict," and that wore is the past tense of the irregular verb wear, which means "to have clothing on."

She said soldiers wore jackets with pockets to hold tools they might need for war survival, not silly things like poetry.

Your Turn Use context clues to distinguish between the meanings of the following homophones from "Shipped Out."

need and **knead**, *page 119* _____

_____

read and **red**, *page 120* _____

_____

CHECK IN ▶ 1 ⟩ 2 ⟩ 3 ⟩ 4 ⟩

Summarize

Summarizing can help readers evaluate details to determine important ideas as they read. It is important to summarize the story in logical order, starting at the beginning, to help you better understand the setting and plot events. Remember that a summary should not include your opinions.

Quick Tip

A summary does not include everything from the story. It should include only the most important information.

 FIND TEXT EVIDENCE

Summarizing the opening paragraphs of "Shipped Out" on page 119 may help you understand the setting and plot elements of the story.

Page 119

> My name is Libby Kendall, and I am a prisoner of war. Well, not really, but some days it feels that way. Just like my dad, I've packed up my things and shipped out. Unlike my dad, however, nothing I do will ever help the Allies win World War II.

The first paragraph introduces Libby Kendall, a girl living during World War II. In the paragraphs that follow, readers learn that because her father has gone off to war and her mother must work long hours, Libby has been sent to live with her Aunt Lucia.

COLLABORATE

Your Turn Summarize what Libby's father plans to do on page 120.

_____

_____

_____

CHECK IN 1 2 3 4

Plot: Flashback

The selection "Shipped Out" is historical fiction. Historical fiction features plot events and settings typical of the past period in which the story takes place. It also features realistic characters who speak and act like people from that period. It may include literary devices such as flashbacks.

🔍 FIND TEXT EVIDENCE

I can tell that "Shipped Out" is historical fiction. The first paragraph mentions a real event, World War II. In a flashback, we learn why Libby, the main character, has to live with her aunt.

Page 120

I remember how intently my parents read reports about the war, which I rarely understood. They often whispered to one another, and I'd shout out something like, "Speak up! I can't hear you!" They'd frown and leave me alone to talk in private.

One night, they came into the living room and turned off the radio. At first I was angry, but they had serious expressions on their faces. "Our country's at war," Dad said. "The military will be looking for new recruits. I know something about boats and ship engines, so I intend to join the navy."

My face grew hot, but my hands felt cold. "You can't just leave," I said. I stomped on the floor for emphasis and stormed off to my bedroom. Looking back on that now, I feel ashamed of how selfishly I had acted.

This morning, Aunt Lucia can tell I'm feeling down. She asks me to help her decorate cupcakes for a fundraiser tonight. At first I'm not interested. I just slather on frosting and plop a berry on top. Then I realize that I can make red stripes out of strawberries and a patch of blue from blueberries. Soon I have a whole tray of cupcakes decorated like flags to show Aunt Lucia.

Flashback

Flashbacks describe events and actions that occurred before the main action of the story. Signal words and phrases, such as *once* or *I remember*, may show a character remembering past events.

COLLABORATE

Your Turn Find the flashback on page 121. How does this flashback differ from the one on page 120?

_____

_____

_____

_____

CHECK IN   1   2   3   4

Theme

To identify a story's **theme,** or overall message, consider what the characters think, say, or do, and analyze the characters' relationships and conflicts. A theme may be stated directly or implied. A story may also have multiple themes. Think about how the characters' perspectives change as a result of what happens to them to help you infer and develop these themes.

Quick Tip

To find a story's theme, you can also think about a lesson a character learns. What the character learns might be a main theme of the story.

 FIND TEXT EVIDENCE

On page 119 of "Shipped Out," Libby says that she feels like a prisoner of war at her aunt's apartment. This is because her father has gone to war and her mother has had to leave for work. Libby feels her efforts are not appreciated, but Aunt Lucia needs her help. These plot events will help me identify the theme.

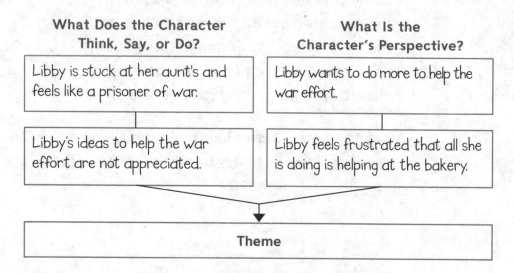

What Does the Character Think, Say, or Do?	What Is the Character's Perspective?
Libby is stuck at her aunt's and feels like a prisoner of war.	Libby wants to do more to help the war effort.
Libby's ideas to help the war effort are not appreciated.	Libby feels frustrated that all she is doing is helping at the bakery.

Theme

 Your Turn What does Libby learn from Aunt Lucia about contributing to the war effort? Add more ideas to the graphic organizer on page 127 to identify a theme of the story.

CHECK IN 1 2 3 4

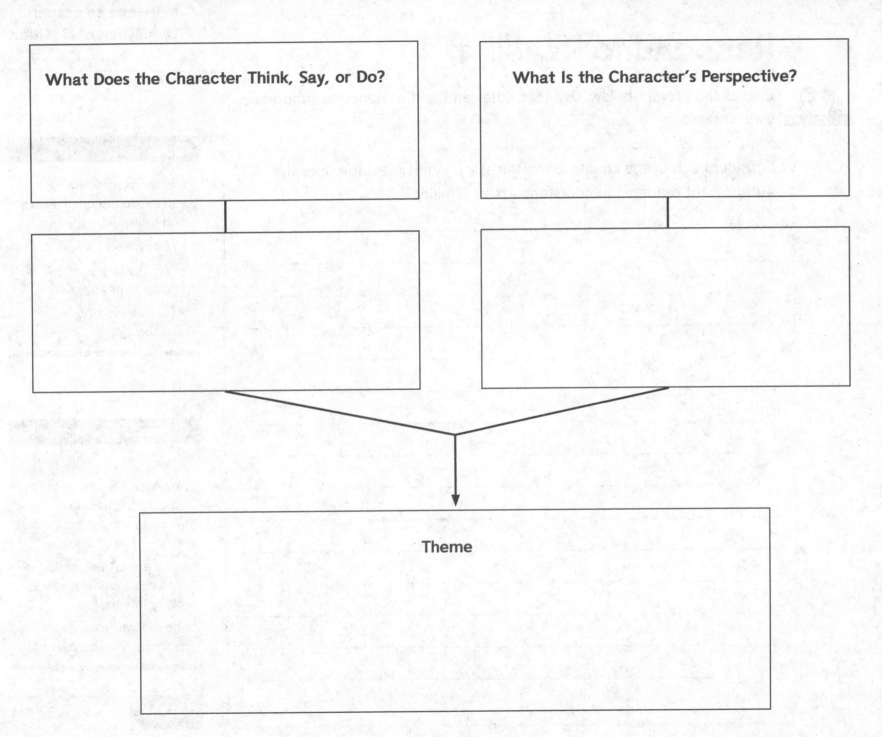

What Does the Character Think, Say, or Do?	What Is the Character's Perspective?

Theme

My Goal I can use text evidence to respond to historical fiction.

Respond to Reading

COLLABORATE

Discuss the prompt below. Use your notes and text evidence to support your answer.

Consider each of the characters in this story. What message does the author want readers to understand about families?

_____

_____

_____

_____

_____

_____

_____

_____

_____

_____

_____

_____

_____

Quick Tip

Use these sentence starters to discuss the text and to organize ideas.

- *Libby feels . . .*
- *Libby's family contributes by . . .*
- *At the end, Libby learns . . .*

Grammar Connections

As you write your response, try to use adverbs to indicate intensity when describing actions. For instance:

*Libby **angrily** responded to the news that her dad was joining the navy.*

*She **thoughtfully** decorated the cupcakes.*

CHECK IN 1 2 3 4

World War II

During World War II, the United States joined the Allies, or the countries fighting the Axis powers, which included the countries of Germany, Italy, and Japan. Choose another Allied country to create a poster that explains how this country contributed to the World War II effort. Work collaboratively with a larger group.

COLLABORATE

Step 1 **Set a Goal** Make a list of the countries in the Allied forces. Consider what happened in these countries before the war started.

Write the name of the country you choose.

_____

Step 2 **Identify Sources** Discuss the print or online sources you will use. Your sources should include relevant information, or information that contains facts, details, and examples about your topic of research. Ask yourself: Does the source include information that is relevant to your audience? Does it support your purpose for writing? If a source does not, you need to find a source that does.

Step 3 **Find and Record Information** To find relevant information, skim and scan the content. Take notes and cite your sources.

What question might you ask about the information you find?

_____

_____

Step 4 **Organize and Synthesize Information** Organize your notes. Decide how to present your information on your poster.

Step 5 **Create and Present** Complete your poster. Present it to the class.

Quick Tip

You can find relevant information in primary and secondary sources. Primary sources can be letters, autobiographies, or newspapers. Secondary sources retell information from primary sources.

Which of these facts would you include as relevant information for a cause of World War II?

- Germany invades Poland in 1939.

- New York World's Fair opens in 1939.

_____

_____

_____

CHECK IN ⟩ 1 ⟩ 2 ⟩ 3 ⟩ 4

The Unbreakable Code

Literature Anthology: pages 430–443

? **Why does Grandfather speak to John in Navajo?**

 Talk About It Reread **Literature Anthology** pages 432 and 433. Discuss with your partner how the Navajo language is described in the selection.

Cite Text Evidence What words and phrases show the effect the Navajo language has on John? Write text evidence in the web.

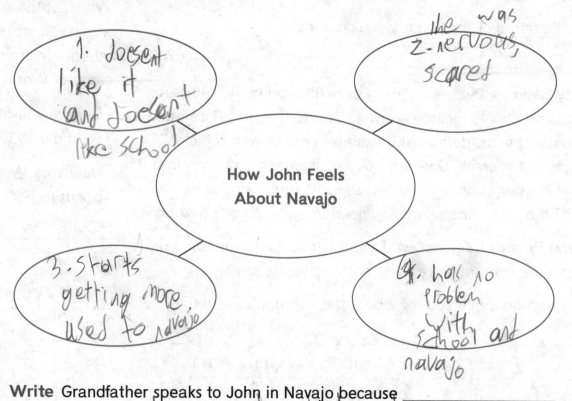

1. doesent like it and doesent like school

the was 2. nervous, scared

How John Feels About Navajo

3. starts getting more used to navajo

4. has no problem with school and navajo

Write Grandfather speaks to John in Navajo because _____
To show and help jhon _____

CHECK IN 1 2 3 4

Why was it important to the story that Grandfather's World War II mission was a secret?

 Talk About It Reread **Literature Anthology** pages 436 and 437. Turn to your partner and discuss how the Navajo code is set up.

Cite Text Evidence What words and phrases tell about the secrecy of Grandfather's mission? Write text evidence.

Text Evidence
Japanese cant break the code.
They could find important info
could find naval bases and airports

↓

Conclusion
Japanese couldnt fin out

Write It was important to the story that Grandfather's World War II mission was a secret because ___It helped the US ant the allied powers win___

Quick Tip

The word *secrecy* means "the action of not letting others know something." Thinking about the meaning of this word will help you find text evidence.

Evaluate Information

The author writes that no information could be passed between American ships, planes, and land forces. How does this information help you understand the importance of secrecy during the war?

CHECK IN 1 > 2 > 3 > 4

? How does John's reaction to his Grandfather's words show how John has changed?

Talk About It Reread **Literature Anthology** page 443. Turn to a partner and discuss how John has changed by the end of the story.

Cite Text Evidence How does Grandfather's story change the way John feels? Cite evidence from the text in your answer.

Grandfather's story shows John

He should be proud of Navajo

↓

John realizes that

he his should language ot with

↓

John is now able to

speak it without restrictions

↓

What these changes tell you about John:

He likes his language

Write By the end of the story, John has changed To be OK with his language and be OK with school

CHECK IN ⟩ 1 ⟩ 2 ⟩ 3 ⟩ 4 ⟩

Respond to Reading

COLLABORATE

Discuss the prompt below. Use your notes and text evidence to support your ideas.

Explain why it was important for Grandfather to share his story with John. Consider the importance from both Grandfather's and John's perspective.

(scribbled out / crossed out text)

so he could be part of his language, and keep the language from dieing out.

Quick Tip

Use these sentence starters to talk about and cite text evidence.

- *The author includes Grandfather's stories to . . .*
- *John's reaction to these stories shows that . . .*
- *In the end, John . . .*

Doug Sherman/Geofile

CHECK IN 1 2 3 4

Allies in Action

Literature Anthology:
pages 446–449

Joining the Allies

[1] Many men left the United States to fight in the war. Women also enlisted, often serving in the Army Nurse Corps. The large number of recruits that went overseas caused a worker shortage back home. In response, many women took jobs previously held by men. They held positions in government and worked in factories. They also raised funds and collected materials that would be recycled into supplies for the troops.

[2] The shortage of workers in agriculture led the United States to institute the Bracero Program with Mexico. Through this program, Mexican laborers worked on farmlands across the United States. These workers helped maintain crops, supporting the country's economy during the war and decades beyond.

Reread paragraph 1. **Underline** a sentence that explains why help from women was needed.

COLLABORATE

Talk with a partner about why the United States needed the help of women and people from other countries.

Evaluate the details in paragraph 2. **Underline** the details that explain how the Bracero Program worked. Explain why the author included this information in the text.

_____

_____

_____

_____

_____

_____

_____

_____

The Tuskegee Airmen

3   By the start of the war, a number of African American men were already active in the military. However, their positions were limited. They were rarely given opportunities for advancement and special military operations.

4   Many civil rights groups had protested these restrictions on African Americans. In response, the U.S. Army Air Corps began a new training program in 1941. They taught African Americans how to become pilots and navigators. This program was based in Tuskegee, Alabama. Those who completed aeronautic, or pilot, training there became known as "The Tuskegee Airmen."

5   The Tuskegee Airmen flew many missions during World War II. Over time, they gained a strong reputation for their skills. Their success would lead the U.S. military to recognize African American service and offer them more training opportunities in different fields.

Circle the sentences that tell you that African American soldiers had limited opportunities.

Draw a box around the sentences that explain what happened as a result.

COLLABORATE

Reread the excerpt on this page. Evaluate the details to determine the important ideas. With a partner, talk about the author's purpose for writing about African Americans in the military during World War II.

Why is it important to know that there were restrictions on African Americans during the war? Use text evidence to support your response.

_____

_____

_____

_____

_____

_____

_____

? **Why did the United States need the contributions of different groups during World War II?**

COLLABORATE

Talk About It Reread the excerpts on pages 134 and 135. Discuss how the different groups helped the United States and the Allies win the war.

Cite Text Evidence Which groups helped contribute to the war effort? What conclusion can we draw by studying these groups?

Synthesize Information

In "Allies in Action," the author mentions a number of groups that contributed to the war effort. Consider why the author chose to use these different groups to make a point.

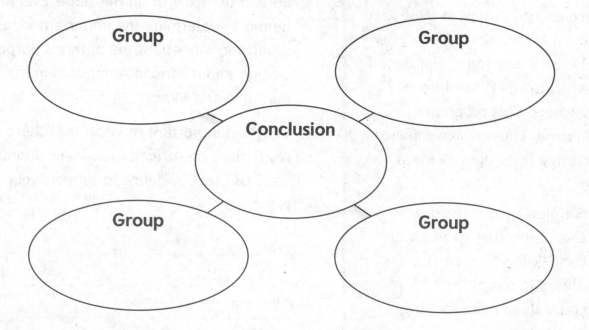

Group

Group

Conclusion

Group

Group

Write The contributions of different groups during the war were needed

because _____

_____

_____

_____

CHECK IN 1 2 3 4

Print and Graphic Features

Authors can choose from many kinds of text features to enhance information and help readers better understand the text. Some of these features are headings, maps, charts, photographs, and captions.

 FIND TEXT EVIDENCE

On pages 448 and 449 of the **Literature Anthology**, the author of "Allies in Action" uses primary source photographs and captions to illustrate the diverse groups who supported the war effort. The caption below describes the photograph shown on the right.

> Nearly 1,000 African Americans completed the pilot training program in Tuskegee, Alabama.

Your Turn Analyze the photograph and caption on page 448.

- What was the author's purpose for using a primary source photo in the text?

  _____

  _____

- How does the caption add to the text?

  _____

  _____

Using visual primary sources will make your writing on historical topics come alive. Primary source photos can show the action and the people involved in an event. They can also provide more specific details that are not included in the main text.

U.S. Air Force photo

CHECK IN ▶ 1 ⟩ 2 ⟩ 3 ⟩ 4

? How is the message of this World War II poster similar to the message of *The Unbreakable Code* and "Allies in Action"?

COLLABORATE

Talk About It Look at the poster and read the caption. Talk with a partner about what the men are doing.

Cite Text Evidence **Underline** clues in the poster that help you understand what the message is. **Circle** evidence in the caption that explains about the poster's purpose.

Write The message of this poster is similar to the message of the selections because

_____

_____

_____

_____

_____

_____

> **Quick Tip**
>
> Talk about contributions people made to the war effort during World War II. Use details in the poster and ideas you read to help you.

Build for Your Navy! This poster was created by Robert Muchley between 1941 and 1942. It encouraged skilled workers to join the Navy during the war.

CHECK IN ⟩ 1 ⟩ 2 ⟩ 3 ⟩ 4 ⟩

My Goal I know how different groups can contribute to a cause.

Write a Newscast

The characters you read about learned different ways to contribute to a cause. Why are all kinds of contributions important to the war effort?

1 Look at your Build Knowledge notes in your reader's notebook.

2 Write a newscast about why all kinds of contributions are important to the war effort. Think about the contributions you read about. Consider how and why the groups accomplished these contributions.

3 Your newscast should follow the 5W and 1H format (who, what, where, when, why, and how). Use the text evidence to support your ideas. Use new vocabulary words.

Think about what you learned in this text set. Fill in the bars on page 117.

Build Knowledge

Essential Question

How are living things adapted to their environment?

Build Vocabulary

Write new words you learned about living things and how they have adapted to their environments. Draw lines and circles for the words you write.

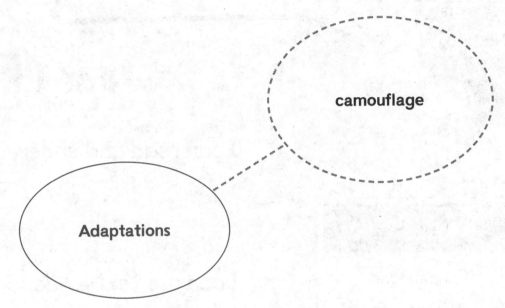

camouflage

Adaptations

Go online to **my.mheducation.com** and read the "Blending In" Blast. Think about the different ways animals adapt to their ecosystems. How do these adaptations help the animals? Then blast back your response.

Think about what you already know. Fill in the bars. Keep doing your best!

Key

1 = I do not understand.

2 = I understand but need more practice.

3 = I understand.

4 = I understand and can teach someone.

What I Know Now

I can read and understand expository text.

1 | 2 | 3 | 4

I can use text evidence to respond to expository text.

1 | 2 | 3 | 4

I know how living things adapt to their environment.

1 | 2 | 3 | 4

STOP You will come back to the next page later.

Think about what you learned. Fill in the bars. You can always improve, so keep trying!

What I Learned

I can read and understand expository text.

| 1 | 2 | 3 | 4 |

I can use text evidence to respond to expository text.

| 1 | 2 | 3 | 4 |

I know how living things adapt to their environment.

| 1 | 2 | 3 | 4 |

My Goal
I can read and understand expository text.

TAKE NOTES

As you read, make note of interesting words and important information.

Neck

Mysterious Oceans

Essential Question

How are living things adapted to their environment?

Read about the adaptation of sea creatures to the deep ocean.

Crabs crawl among giant tube worms in the deep ocean. New ocean species are being discovered all the time.

Emory Kristof/National Geographic Stock

Deep Diving

It has no mouth, eyes, or stomach. Its soft body is encased in a white cylinder and topped with a red plume. It can grow to be eight feet tall. It is a sea creature known as a giant tube worm, and it lives without any sunlight on the deep, dark ocean floor.

What we sometimes call the deep ocean, in contrast to shallow waters, covers almost two-thirds of Earth's surface. On average, oceans are about two miles deep. However, the deepest point known on Earth, Challenger Deep, descends nearly seven miles.

The ocean's floor is varied, consisting of vast plains, steep canyons, and towering mountains. It includes active, **dormant**, and extinct volcanoes. This undersea world is a harsh environment because of its **frigid** temperatures and lack of sunshine.

The deep ocean is also a mysterious environment that remains largely unexplored. Little is known about it or its creatures. Do any of them **cache** food the way land animals do? Do any ocean species **hibernate**? As one example among countless mysteries, not a single, live giant squid had ever been spotted until a few years ago. We knew they existed only because their corpses had been found.

The Challenger Deep is located in an undersea canyon called the Mariana Trench.

The Deepest Known Point on Earth

CHINA   JAPAN   PACIFIC OCEAN

PHILIPPINES

0 km   1,000
0 miles   1,000
Miller Projection

Key

Mariana Trench
1,554 miles long
and 44 miles wide

● Challenger Deep

FIND TEXT EVIDENCE

Read

Paragraphs 1-2

Ask and Answer Questions

What is a question you can ask and answer about the ocean? Write the question and underline the answer.

_____

_____

Paragraphs 3-4

Cause and Effect

Circle the text that tells why the deep ocean is a harsh environment.

Map

Look at the map. In what ocean is the Mariana Trench located?

_____

_____

Reread

Author's Craft

Why do you think the author begins the text by describing a sea creature?

This fish, the striated frogfish, lures prey. The nose is an adaptation to life in the deep ocean.

A basket starfish rests in a deep sea coral reef.

FIND TEXT EVIDENCE 🔍

Read

Paragraphs 1-3

Cause and Effect

What allowed scientists to begin exploring the deep ocean floor?

_____

_____

_____

Draw a box around the effect of this exploration.

Paragraph 4

Context Clues

How do context clues help you to determine the meaning of *bioluminescent*?

_____

_____

Reread

Author's Craft

How do the photographs and captions support the text? What do they help you understand?

Amazing Adaptations

When a submersible, or submarine, was invented that could descend farther than any other craft, scientists were then able to make the odyssey to the deep ocean floor. However, exploration remains difficult, and they have since seen merely five percent of the underwater world.

As scientists anticipated, life generally seems sparse at the bottom of the deep ocean. Few creatures can survive there. Food sources that sea creatures depend on, such as dead plants and animals, rarely drift down from the ocean's surface. As a result, animals have to adapt to an environment that is not only frigid and dark but also has little food.

One example of an **adaptation** to this environment is seen in the starfish. Deep sea starfish grow larger and more aggressive than their shallow water relatives. They can't afford to wait for an occasional snail to pass by. Instead, deep sea starfish are predators that actively **forage** for food. They reach up their five arms, which have pincers at the ends, to catch meals of **agile**, fast-moving shrimp.

Anglerfish also are adapted to the herculean task of finding scarce food. Each has a bioluminescent, or naturally glowing, lure on the top of its head. This shining pole is sensitive to vibrations and allows them to attract other fish. With their huge jaws, they quickly seize their prey.

Heated Habitats

What has truly surprised scientists, however, is the discovery of another, very different type of environment on the deep ocean floor. They found that cracks, or vents, in Earth's surface exist underwater, just as they do on dry land. Sea water rushes into these vents, where it mingles with chemicals. The water is also heated by magma, or hot melted rock. When the water from the vent bursts back into the ocean, it creates geysers and hot springs.

To scientists' amazement, the habitats around these vents teem with life. In addition to tube worms, there are huge clams, eyeless shrimp, crabs, and mussels, along with many kinds of bacteria. One odd creature is the Pompeii worm. It has a fleece of bacteria on its back that, as far as scientists can determine, **insulates** it from heat.

How can so much life exist where there is so little food or sunlight? Scientists have discovered that many creatures transform the chemicals from the vents into food. The process is called chemosynthesis. Because of this process, animals are able to flourish in these remarkable habitats. Creatures that don't use chemosynthesis for food, such as crabs, eat the ones that do.

There are many mysteries to be found and solved at the bottom of the deep sea. In the last few decades alone, scientists have discovered more than 1,500 ocean species! If scientists continue sea exploration, they are bound to discover many more.

Summarize

Use your notes to orally summarize the central idea and relevant ideas you learned about in "Mysterious Oceans."

FIND TEXT EVIDENCE

Read

Paragraphs 1–4

Ask and Answer Questions

What is a question you can ask and answer to check your comprehension of this section? Underline the answer to your question.

_____

_____

_____

_____

_____

_____

_____

Reread

Author's Craft

How does the author help you visualize life around the vents in the deep ocean?

Vocabulary

Use the example sentences to talk with a partner about each word. Then answer the questions.

adaptation

Changing color is an **adaptation** some lizards have made to their environments.

How is fur an example of an adaptation?

_____

_____

agile

Kim was such an **agile** gymnast, she could do a backbend on a balance beam.

Why should athletes be agile?

_____

_____

cache

My parents **cache** jewelry and other treasures in a box in our basement.

Where else might people cache special things?

_____

_____

dormant

The guide explained that the volcano was **dormant**, so we felt safe standing near it.

Why is it safe to visit a dormant volcano?

not an active volcano

_____

forage

When winter comes, elk, deer, and other animals often must **forage** for food.

Why is it hard to forage for food during winter?

They won't have enough food to eat.

Build Your Word List Reread the first paragraph on page 146. Circle the word *invented*. In your reader's notebook, use a word web to write more forms of the word. For example, *inventor*. Use an online or print dictionary to check for accuracy.

frigid

We drank a hot beverage to warm up after being outside on a **frigid** day.

Do you usually wear shorts in frigid weather?

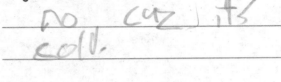

No, cuz its cold.

hibernate

Some animals, such as the dormouse, **hibernate** during the winter.

Why do some animals hibernate in the winter?

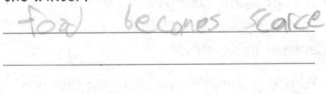

Food becones scarce

insulates

My coat **insulates** my body against the cold.

What insulates a cat against the cold?

Fur Protects them from cold

Context Clues

If you read an unfamiliar or multiple-meaning word, you can look for clues to its meaning in the paragraph in which it appears.

🔍 FIND TEXT EVIDENCE

In the first paragraph of "Mysterious Oceans" on page 145, I see the word cylinder. *I'm not sure what* cylinder *means. Since the creature being discussed is called a* tube worm, *I think a cylinder may refer to the tube around the worm.*

Its soft body is encased in a white cylinder and topped with a red plume. It can grow to be eight feet tall. It is a sea creature known as a giant tube worm, and it lives without any sunlight on the deep, dark ocean floor.

Your Turn Use context clues to find the meaning of these words in "Mysterious Oceans."

sparse, *page 146* _____

_____

aggressive, *page 146* _____

CHECK IN ⟩ 1 ⟩ 2 ⟩ 3 ⟩ 4 ⟩

Emory Kristof/National Geographic Stock

Ask and Answer Questions

Asking and answering questions can help you monitor your comprehension of complex scientific text. This can also help deepen your understanding of the topic. You can ask yourself what the central, or main, ideas are or reasons for a statement. You can reread parts of the text to find the answers and increase your understanding.

 FIND TEXT EVIDENCE

The last paragraph in the section "Deep Diving" on page 145 of "Mysterious Oceans" asks several questions about oceans. You may wonder why these questions are being asked.

Quick Tip

Begin the questions you ask yourself with these words:

Who_____?

What _____?

Where _____?

When _____?

Why _____?

How _____?

Page 145

The deep ocean is also a mysterious environment that remains largely unexplored. Little is known about it or its creatures. Do any of them **cache** food the way land animals do? Do any ocean species **hibernate**? As one example among countless mysteries, not a single, live giant squid had ever been spotted until a few years ago. We knew they existed only because their corpses had been found.

There must be reasons why we know so little about ocean life. I'm going to ask myself, "Why is the deep ocean so mysterious?" I will reread the section to try to answer this question.

COLLABORATE

Your Turn Use the information in the first two paragraphs of "Deep Diving" on page 145 to answer the question "Why is the deep ocean so mysterious?"

_____

_____

_____

_____

CHECK IN 1 2 3 4

Maps

The selection "Mysterious Oceans" is expository text. Expository text presents information about a topic. It presents central ideas that are supported by relevant details. It may be structured to show cause-and-effect relationships. The authors of expository texts may include text features such as photos, captions, and maps.

FIND TEXT EVIDENCE

I can tell "Mysterious Oceans" is expository text. The text gives information about oceans. It presents central ideas and is organized with cause-and-effect relationships. A map gives visual information.

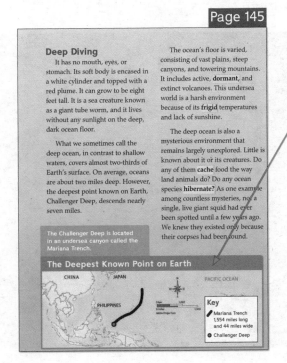

Page 145

Deep Diving

It has no mouth, eyes, or stomach. Its soft body is encased in a white cylinder and topped with a red plume. It can grow to be eight feet tall. It is a sea creature known as a giant tube worm, and it lives without any sunlight on the deep, dark ocean floor.

What we sometimes call the deep ocean, in contrast to shallow waters, covers almost two-thirds of Earth's surface. On average, oceans are about two miles deep. However, the deepest point known on Earth, Challenger Deep, descends nearly seven miles.

The ocean's floor is varied, consisting of vast plains, steep canyons, and towering mountains. It includes active, **dormant**, and extinct volcanoes. This undersea world is a harsh environment because of its **frigid** temperatures and lack of sunshine.

The deep ocean is also a mysterious environment that remains largely unexplored. Little is known about it or its creatures. Do any of them **cache** food the way land animals do? Do any ocean species **hibernate**? As one example among countless mysteries, not a single, live giant squid had ever been spotted until a few years ago. We knew they existed only because their corpses had been found.

The Challenger Deep is located in an undersea canyon called the Mariana Trench.

The Deepest Known Point on Earth

CHINA   JAPAN   PACIFIC OCEAN

PHILIPPINES

Key
▲ Mariana Trench
1,554 miles long
and 44 miles wide
● Challenger Deep

Map

A map is a flat picture of an area. Most maps have a title, a scale to show how many miles are represented, a compass rose to show directions, and a key that explains colors or symbols.

Your Turn Study the map on page 145. What is the approximate length and width of the Mariana Trench? How does the map help you visualize it?

_____

_____

_____

CHECK IN 1 2 3 4

Cause and Effect

To figure out cause-and-effect relationships in a text, first look for an event or action that makes something happen. This is the **cause**. Then look for what happens as a result of that cause. This is the **effect**. Words and phrases such as *because of, as a result, if/then,* or *when* can signal cause and effect.

FIND TEXT EVIDENCE

In the first paragraph of the section "Amazing Adaptations" on page 146 of "Mysterious Oceans," the author explains that a new type of submersible was invented. The word when *signals a cause-and-effect relationship. This invention caused something else to happen.*

Cause	⟶	Effect
Invention of submersible	⟶	Exploration of ocean floor

Your Turn Reread the rest of the section "Amazing Adaptations" on page 146. Identify the cause-and-effect relationships explained in these paragraphs and list them in your graphic organizer on page 153.

Lophelia II 2009 Expedition, NOAA-OER

Quick Tip

To identify cause-and effect relationships, ask yourself these questions:

What happened?

Why did it happen?

The answer to *Why did it happen?* is the cause.

The answer to *What happened?* is the effect.

CHECK IN 1 2 3 4

Cause	$\longrightarrow$	Effect
	$\longrightarrow$	
	$\longrightarrow$	
	$\longrightarrow$	
	$\longrightarrow$	

My Goal: **I can use text evidence to respond to expository text.**

Respond to Reading

COLLABORATE

Discuss the prompt below. Use your notes and text evidence to support your response.

Why has so little of the deep sea been explored? Why is deep sea exploration important?

_____

_____

_____

_____

_____

_____

_____

_____

_____

_____

_____

_____

_____

_____

_____

CHECK IN 1 > 2 > 3 > 4 >

Animal Adaptation

Many animals have adaptations that help them survive in their environment. Choose some of these animal adaptations to create a multimedia slideshow. Work collaboratively with a partner.

Step 1 **Set a Goal** Narrow your focus. Which animal adaptations would you like to learn more about?

_____

Step 2 **Identify Sources** To research multimedia information about animal adaptations, it is easiest to do so online. Discuss the websites you will use. Decide how to divide the research so you can quickly find details that support your topic.

Step 3 **Find and Record Information** Take notes and cite your sources. How are the adaptations of the animals similar or different from other animal groups? Think about the videos, photos, sound effects, and music clips you found. Then plan what to include. The multimedia elements you choose can emphasize specific ideas. What else would you need to think about when planning a multimedia slideshow?

_____

Step 4 **Organize and Synthesize Information** Organize your notes. Be sure to properly cite the multimedia elements you are using.

Step 5 **Create and Present** After you complete your slideshow, present your work to the class.

The desert fox lives in a hot environment. Its large ears help to release heat to keep the body cool.

The photo and caption above show an example of an animal adaptation.

Tech Tip

If you are having problems finding appropriate photos, try using different key words.

CHECK IN ⟩ 1 ⟩ 2 ⟩ 3 ⟩ 4

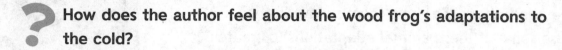

Survival at 40 Below

? How does the author feel about the wood frog's adaptations to the cold?

Literature Anthology: pages 450–465

COLLABORATE

Talk About It Reread **Literature Anthology** page 453. Turn to your partner and discuss how the author talks about how frogs change in order to survive the Arctic.

Cite Text Evidence How does the author help you understand how she feels about how the frog adapts to the Arctic? Write text evidence.

Make Inferences

You can often infer how the author feels about a subject by paying attention to the author's word choice. Think about the words the author uses to describe the wood frog and what it does. Are they words that give a positive feeling or a negative feeling? Based on her word choice, what inferences can you make about the author's feelings toward the wood frog?

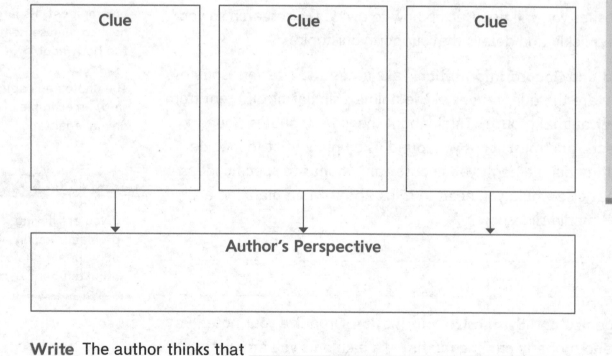

Clue	Clue	Clue

Author's Perspective

Write The author thinks that _____

_____

_____

CHECK IN 1 > 2 > 3 > 4 >

? **Why does the author describe the arctic fox as an acrobat?**

COLLABORATE

Talk About It Reread **Literature Anthology** page 457. Notice that the author uses a simile to compare the arctic fox and an acrobat. Turn to your partner and discuss how the arctic fox is like an acrobat and how it is not.

Cite Text Evidence How are the arctic fox and an acrobat alike and different? Write text evidence in the diagram.

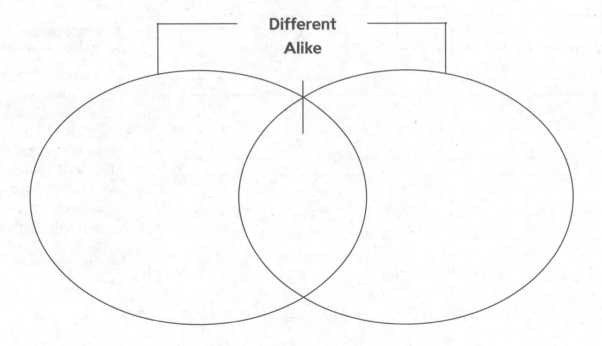

Different

Alike

Write The author describes the arctic fox as an acrobat _____

_____

_____

_____

CHECK IN 1 2 3 4

? **How does the author use sensory language to paint a picture with words on page 463?**

Talk About It Reread **Literature Anthology** page 463. Turn to a partner and talk about what the Arctic is like at the beginning of spring.

Cite Text Evidence What words and phrases help you picture what spring is like in the Arctic? Write text evidence.

Text Evidence	I Visualize

Write The author uses sensory language to paint a picture _____

_____

_____

_____

_____

CHECK IN 1 2 3 4

Respond to Reading

COLLABORATE

Discuss the prompt below. Use your notes and text evidence to support your answer.

What makes the Arctic an area that biologists are especially interested in studying? What might happen to environments like the Arctic if wildlife were unable to adapt?

_____

_____

_____

_____

_____

_____

_____

_____

_____

_____

Quick Tip

Use these sentence starters to talk about and cite text evidence.

- *The Arctic's harsh environment means that . . .*
- *Arctic animals are special because . . .*
- *Without the ability to adapt, Arctic animals might . . .*

USFWS/Donna Dewhurst

CHECK IN 1 2 3 4

Why the Evergreen Trees Never Lose Their Leaves

Literature Anthology:
pages 468–471

1   "No, indeed," answered the birch-tree, drawing her fair leaves away. "We of the great forest have our own birds to help. I can do nothing for you."

2   "The birch is not very strong," said the little bird to itself, "and it might be that she could not hold me easily. I will ask the oak." So the bird said, "Great oak-tree, you are so strong, will you not let me live on your boughs till my friends come back in the springtime?"

3   "In the springtime!" cried the oak. "That is a long way off. How do I know what you might do in all that time? Birds are always looking for something to eat, and you might even eat up some of my acorns."

Reread the excerpt. **Circle** the lines of dialogue that tell you something about the trees' characters. Write what it reveals about the trees.

_____

_____

COLLABORATE

Talk with a partner about what you can infer about the little bird from his reaction to the birch-tree. **Underline** the words in paragraph 2 that tell you his reaction.

1   "Come right here, then," said the friendly spruce-tree, for it was her voice that had called. "You shall live on my warmest branch all winter if you choose."

2   "Will you really let me?" asked the little bird eagerly.

3   "Indeed, I will," answered the kind-hearted spruce-tree. "If your friends have flown away, it is time for the trees to help you. Here is the branch where my leaves are thickest and softest."

4   "My branches are not very thick," said the friendly pine-tree, "but I am big and strong, and I can keep the north wind from you and the spruce."

5   "I can help too," said a little juniper-tree. "I can give you berries all winter long, and every bird knows that juniper berries are good."

Reread the excerpt. **Underline** the sentence in paragraph 1 that tells what the spruce-tree offers the little bird.

Underline the sentence in paragraph 5 that tells what the juniper-tree offers the little bird.

COLLABORATE

Talk about the trees with a partner. How do they respond to the bird? **Circle** words that show what the trees are like.

What do these trees do? Use text evidence to support your response.

_____

_____

_____

_____

_____

? **Why does the author contrast the behavior of the two groups of trees?**

COLLABORATE

Talk About It Reread the excerpts on pages 160 and 161. With a partner, discuss the different groups of trees. How are they different?

Cite Text Evidence What words and phrases describe the behavior of the two groups of trees? Write what it tells you about the trees.

Text Evidence	→	What It Tells
	→	
	→	
	→	
	→	

Write The author shows the two groups of trees differently because _____
_____
_____

Quick Tip

As you reread, think about what the behavior of each tree means. Take notes on a piece of paper. Use your notes to help you fill in the chart.

CHECK IN 1 2 3 4

Character Perspective

An author uses third-person point of view to develop a character's **perspective**, or attitude. In third-person point of view, the narrator is not in the story. In third-person limited point of view, the narrator knows the thoughts and feelings of only one character. Identifying a character's point of view can help you understand how the character's perspective has changed from the beginning to the end of a story.

 FIND TEXT EVIDENCE

In "Why the Evergreen Trees Never Lose Their Leaves," the author tells the story in third-person limited point of view, focusing on the little bird. In paragraph 2 on page 160, the words "said the little bird to itself" show that the narrator knows the bird's thoughts and feelings.

> "The birch is not very strong," said the little bird to itself, "and it might be that she could not hold me easily. I will ask the oak." So the bird said, "Great oak-tree, you are so strong, will you not let me live on your boughs till my friends come back in the springtime?"

COLLABORATE

Your Turn Reread paragraphs 1 and 2 on page 160.

- How do you know the point of view is third-person limited?

  _____

  _____

- How do the bird's words to the oak-tree show her perspective?

  _____

  _____

Readers to Writers

If you choose to write from a third-person limited point of view, the narrator will tell the thoughts and feelings of only one character. Other characters may say how they feel or express a thought through dialogue. In a first-person point of view, the narrator takes part in the actions of the story and refers to himself or herself as *I*.

CHECK IN 1 2 3 4

Integrate | **MAKE CONNECTIONS**

? How are the adaptations you see in this photograph similar to the adaptations described in *Survival at 40 Below* and "Why the Evergreen Trees Never Lose Their Leaves"?

Talk About It Look at the photograph and read the caption. With a partner, talk about what you see and how this animal has adapted to its habitat.

Cite Text Evidence **Draw a box** around details that help show the setting of the photograph. **Circle** the hare's adaptations. **Underline** evidence in the caption that tells more about how this animal adapts. Think about how these adaptations help the hare survive its environment.

Write The adaptations in this photograph are

similar to the ones in the selections because _____

_____

_____

_____

_____

_____

_____

> **Quick Tip**
>
> Look back at the two texts in the question and list the adaptations described in them. Then, compare those adaptations to the ones in the photograph.

Can you see this snowshoe hare? His fur turns white in winter. During summer months, this animal is brown. It takes 10 weeks for its fur to change completely.

CHECK IN ⟩ 1 ⟩ 2 ⟩ 3 ⟩ 4 ⟩

My Goal I know how living things adapt to their environment.

Write a Magazine Article

You read about how living things survive in their unique ecosystems. But how do changes in environment affect their survival?

1 Look at your Build Knowledge notes in your reader's notebook.

2 Write a magazine article that answers the following question: Why are adaptations necessary for survival in extreme or unusual environments?

3 Give examples from the texts to support your ideas. Use new vocabulary words.

Think about what you learned in this text set. Fill in the bars on page 143.

Build Knowledge

Essential Question

What can our connections to the world teach us?

Build Vocabulary

Write new words you learned about ways to stay connected to our friends, our families, our communities, and our cultures. Draw lines and circles for the words you write.

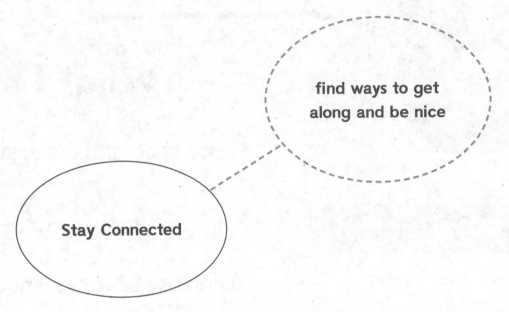

find ways to get along and be nice

Stay Connected

Go online to **my.mheducation.com** and read the "Be Nice" Blast. Think about how being nice helps people to get along. Then blast back your response.

Think about what you already know. Fill in the bars. We all do better with practice.

Key

1 = I do not understand.

2 = I understand but need more practice.

3 = I understand.

4 = I understand and can teach someone.

What I Know Now

I can read and understand poetry.

| 1 | 2 | 3 | 4 |

I can use text evidence to respond to poetry.

| 1 | 2 | 3 | 4 |

I know what our connections to the world can teach us.

| 1 | 2 | 3 | 4 |

STOP You will come back to the next page later.

Think about what you learned.
Fill in the bars. Good job!

What I Learned

I can read and understand poetry.

1 2 3 4

I can use text evidence to respond to poetry.

1 2 3 4

I know what our connections to the
world can teach us.

1 2 3 4

My Goal I can read and understand poetry.

TAKE NOTES

As you read, make note of interesting words and important details.

_____

_____

_____

_____

_____

_____

_____

_____

_____

_____

_____

To Travel!

To travel! To travel!
To visit distant places;
To leave my corner of the world
To seek new names and faces.
Adventure! Adventure!
Exploring foreign lands;
If I can leap across the globe,
My universe expands!

A novel waves her arms to me,
"Come read! Come read!" she cries.
Her pages dance with ancient tales,
A feast for hungry eyes!
The paintings on museum walls
Are begging me to tour:
"Leave your home and live our scenes,
A grand exchange for sure!"

Essential Question

What can our connections to the world teach us?

Read two poems about connecting with other cultures and with nature.

Peter Zelei/Getty Images

To travel! To travel!
Through timeless books and art,
I enter and experience
A life so far apart.

I sail across the seven seas,
My heart soars like a bird.
And soon I'm hearing languages
I've never, ever heard.

Far across the seven seas,
Aromas fill the air.
Foods I've never, ever tried
Are eaten everywhere!
Music blares a different tune,
And strange, new clothes are worn.
Parents pass on customs
To the young ones who are born.

I've traveled! I've traveled!
It's left me more aware;
A valuable connection
To the universe we share.
By reading books and viewing art,
I've learned a thing or two:
The world was made not just for me,
But made for me and you!

—Jad Abbas

FIND TEXT EVIDENCE

Read

Page 170

Personification

Circle text in the second stanza that describes what the paintings want the speaker to do. What does this help you to know?

_____

_____

_____

Pages 170–171

Make Inferences

What does the speaker think of reading books and viewing art?

_____

_____

_____

_____

Reread

Author's Craft

How does the poet use a simile, a comparison using _like_ or _as_, to show the speaker's feelings?

FIND TEXT EVIDENCE 🔍

Read

Page 172

Assonance and Consonance

Circle four words in the third line that show assonance, or the repetition of the same vowel sound in two or more words. What feelings do the sounds contribute to the poem?

Page 172

Point of View and Perspective

Underline a detail that gives you a clue about what the speaker thinks about her grandmother's actions. How does the speaker feel?

Reread

Author's Craft

What can you infer about the speaker from the last two sentences on this page? What words and phrases helped you make your inference?

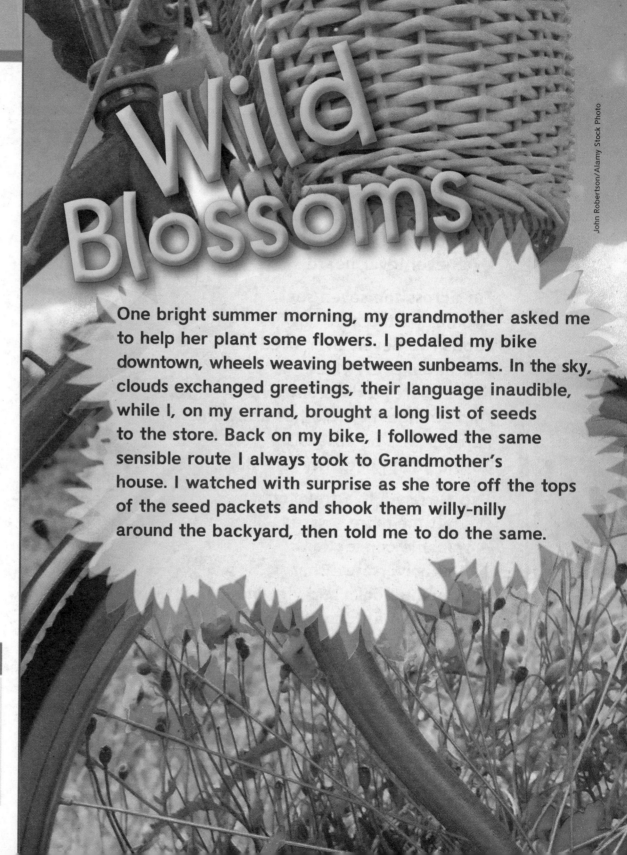

Wild Blossoms

John Robertson/Alamy Stock Photo

One bright summer morning, my grandmother asked me to help her plant some flowers. I pedaled my bike downtown, wheels weaving between sunbeams. In the sky, clouds exchanged greetings, their language inaudible, while I, on my errand, brought a long list of seeds to the store. Back on my bike, I followed the same sensible route I always took to Grandmother's house. I watched with surprise as she tore off the tops of the seed packets and shook them willy-nilly around the backyard, then told me to do the same.

"I thought we were planting a garden," I told her,
"with row after row of flowers." She said, "Oh, no!
I prefer a mountain meadow, one with plenty
of variety." As she talked, bees buzzed about
in excitable flight, impatient for blossoms.
Quick swifts and happy sparrows dipped, dove, and darted
after the falling seeds. My grandmother and I
danced about the backyard, arms outstretched, letting seeds
loose on the wind, joyfully dreaming of the wild
beauty that would fill the yard, and us, all summer.

—Amelia Campos

Make Connections

How do the connections described
in the poems compare with your
own experiences?

FIND TEXT EVIDENCE 🔍

Read

Pages 172–173
Narrative Poetry

How do you know this is a narrative
poem, one that tells a story?

_____

_____

_____

Page 173
Point of View and Perspective

By the end, what is the speaker's
perspective, or how she feels,
about her grandmother's planting?

_____

_____

Underline the details that helped
you find your answer.

Reread

Author's Craft

Look at the third and fourth
sentences on this page. How does
the poet's use of imagery help you
visualize what the speaker is seeing?

Vocabulary

Use the example sentences to talk with a partner about each word. Then answer the questions.

blares

When a trumpet **blares**, Frankie covers his ears.

What might be the reason why someone blares music?

_____

_____

connection

Ron feels a strong **connection** to the players on his soccer team.

How would you establish a connection with a new friend?

_____

_____

errand

My mom sent me on an **errand** to mail a letter.

What errand would you do for a friend or a relative?

_____

_____

exchange

Milo and his brothers were paid ten dollars in **exchange** for shoveling snow.

What favor might you do in exchange for free movie tickets?

_____

_____

Poetry Terms

personification

Poets use **personification** to make objects, animals, or ideas resemble people.

How might personification help describe a thunderstorm?

_____

_____

assonance

A poem using **assonance** includes words with the same vowel sound.

List three words that have assonance with the word *moon*.

_____

_____

consonance

A poem with **consonance** has words with the same middle or final consonant sound.

Name three words that have consonance with the word *home*.

_____

_____

imagery

With **imagery**, poets use words to create a vivid picture.

What imagery might you use to describe a rainy day?

_____

_____

_____

Build Your Word List Pick a word you found interesting in either poem. Look up the word's meaning and origin, or the language it comes from, in a print or online dictionary. Write the word and its meaning and origin in your reader's notebook.

Personification

Personification is a type of figurative language. **Personification** is the use of human characteristics to describe nonhuman things, such as animals, objects, or ideas. Poets use personification to create vivid images and to help the reader picture a detail or understand an idea.

FIND TEXT EVIDENCE

In "To Travel!" a novel is described as a person waving her arms and crying, "Come read!" The pages "dance" and eyes are described as "hungry." These human descriptions make books and their contents seem exciting and alive for the reader.

A novel waves her arms to me,
"Come read! Come read!" she cries.
Her pages dance with ancient tales,
A feast for hungry eyes!

Your Turn How is personification used to describe clouds in "Wild Blossoms"? What is the effect of this?

_____

_____

CHECK IN 1 2 3 4

Assonance and Consonance

Quick Tip

If you are unsure if a vowel is making a long sound, look the word up in a dictionary. A line above a vowel means it has a long sound. This means the letter sounds like its name. For example, $\bar{a}$ as in *pāge*.

Poets may repeat sounds in words for emphasis or effect. **Assonance** is the repetition of the same vowel sound in two or more words. **Consonance** is the repetition of a final or middle consonant sound. The sounds contribute to a poem's feeling.

FIND TEXT EVIDENCE

Reread the poem "To Travel!" on pages 170 and 171. Look for examples of assonance and consonance.

Page 170

> A novel waves her arms to me,
> "Come read! Come read!" she cries.
> Her pages dance with ancient tales,
> A feast for hungry eyes!
> The paintings on museum walls
> Are begging me to tour:
> "Leave your home and live our scenes,
> A grand exchange for sure!"

The long a sound in pages, ancient, *and* tales *is repeated to emphasize the contents of the novel. The repetition of the /z/ sound in the words* pages, tales, eyes, paintings, museum, walls, *and* scenes *creates a feeling of how much there is to see and do.*

Your Turn Find examples of assonance and consonance in "Wild Blossoms" on page 173. Say the words in those lines aloud. What feelings do the sounds contribute to the poem?

_____

_____

_____

CHECK IN ⟩ 1 ⟩ 2 ⟩ 3 ⟩ 4 ⟩

Lyric and Narrative

Lyric poetry expresses personal thoughts and feelings. It has a musical quality and may include rhyme and rhythm. It often contains imagery.

Narrative poetry tells a story and sometimes has characters and dialogue. It may have meter and often contains imagery.

Readers to Writers

When you write about a poem, remember to distinguish between the poet and the speaker. The poet is the author of the poem. The speaker is the narrator or voice telling the poem.

FIND TEXT EVIDENCE

I can tell that "To Travel!" is a lyric poem expressing the speaker's personal feelings. "Wild Blossoms" is a narrative poem that tells a story. Both poems contain imagery, or words that help readers create mental images and deepen their understanding.

Page 171

To travel! To travel!
Through timeless books and art,
I enter and experience
A life so far apart.

I sail across the seven seas,
My heart soars like a bird.
And soon I'm hearing languages
I've never, ever heard.

Far across the seven seas,
Aromas fill the air.
Foods I've never, ever tried
Are eaten everywhere!
Music blares a different tune,
And strange, new clothes are worn.
Parents pass on customs
To the young ones who are born.

I've traveled! I've traveled!
It's left me more aware;
A valuable connection
To the universe we share.
By reading books and viewing art,
I've learned a thing or two:
The world was made not just for me,
But made for me and you!

— Jad Abbas

"To Travel!" is a lyric poem. The line *My heart soars like a bird* expresses the speaker's feelings about traveling the world. The line *I sail across the seven seas* shows imagery of traveling.

COLLABORATE

Your Turn Compare the way the speakers of "To Travel!" and "Wild Blossoms" express themselves. How are the poems similar and different?

_____

_____

_____

_____

_____

CHECK IN 1 2 3 4

Point of View and Perspective

The **point of view** refers to who is telling the story or poem. **Perspective** is the attitude the speaker of the poem feels or thinks about an idea. Notice details such as the strong descriptive words that the speaker expresses in his or her point of view. Poets use these details to develop the speaker's perspective.

 FIND TEXT EVIDENCE

"To Travel!" and "Wild Blossoms" are written in the first-person point of view. I'll reread "To Travel!" to look for details that help me figure out the speaker's perspective.

Details	Speaker's Perspective
If I can leap across the globe, My universe expands!	The speaker is excited, curious, and open-minded about the world.
Her pages dance with ancient tales, A feast for hungry eyes!	
I've traveled! I've traveled! It's left me more aware.	

 Your Turn Reread the poem "Wild Blossoms." List important details in the graphic organizer on page 179. Use the details to figure out the speaker's perspective.

List important details in the graphic organizer on page 179.

Quick Tip

As you reread "Wild Blossoms," look for sentences in which the speaker uses first-person point of view, or where the pronoun *I* is used. Think about how these sentences reveal the speaker's perspective.

CHECK IN 1 2 3 4

Details	Speaker's Perspective

My Goal I can use text evidence to respond to poetry.

Respond to Reading

COLLABORATE Discuss the prompt below. Use your notes and text evidence to respond to your ideas.

How does each poet's use of imagery relate to his or her message?

_____

_____

_____

_____

_____

_____

_____

_____

_____

_____

_____

_____

_____

_____

_____

_____

_____

_____

Quick Tip

Use these sentence starters to paraphrase the poems and organize ideas.

- In "To Travel!," the poet uses imagery to describe . . .

- In "Wild Blossoms," the poet uses imagery to describe . . .

- The speaker says . . .

- In both poems, the poets use imagery to . . .

Grammar Connections

As you write your response, be sure to use present tense verbs when talking about the poem. For example:

The poet **uses** imagery to show . . .

These images **show** . . .

The speaker **says** . . .

CHECK IN 1 > 2 > 3 > 4 >

Connections

We can show that we connect to people in our community. Research an important issue that impacts other people in your community, town, or state. Then write an email to send to an elected official or appointed leader in your local community, town, or state government. Work collaboratively with a partner.

Step 1 **Set a Goal** Discuss why sending an email is a good way to contact government leaders about an issue. How are an email and a letter alike and different? Write your answer.

_____

_____

Step 2 **Identify Sources** Discuss the issues that are important to you. Consider how these issues impact others in your community, town, or state. Then choose one issue to research. Discuss how to find the most accurate and up-to-date information in the print or online sources you will use.

Step 3 **Find and Record Information** Take notes, including the best person to contact about the issue. Cite your sources.

Step 4 **Organize and Synthesize Information** Organize your notes into a draft. Be sure to use appropriate, respectful, and formal language. State the issue you want to address. Explain why you want to address it, and include the information you gathered.

Step 5 **Create and Present** Create a final version of your email. Use the correct salutation, or greeting, when addressing the person you are contacting. Then present your email to your class.

  School Crosswalk

To: andrea.ruiz@example.gov

Subject: School Crosswalk

Dear Mayor Ruiz:

We are students in Ms. Scott's fifth grade class at Madison Elementary. There is a busy crosswalk in front of our school. We would like information about getting a traffic light put in at the intersection.

The sample email above shows the beginning of a message that describes a community issue.

CHECK IN 1 ⟩ 2 ⟩ 3 ⟩ 4

You Are My Music

 How does the poet use words and phrases to describe what Ana means to her sister, Aida?

Literature Anthology: pages 472–474

 Talk About It Reread the first and last stanzas on **Literature Anthology** pages 472–473. Talk with a partner about how Aida describes Ana.

Cite Text Evidence What details in the poem help you understand the connection between Ana's hands and her sister? Write text evidence.

Text Evidence	What It Tells About Ana

Write Aida describes Ana's hands _____

_____

_____

Make Inferences

Pay attention to how Aida describes Ana's hands and what the hands are doing. Does she use words that are positive or negative? Paying attention to the feeling a word or phrase gives will help you infer how the speaker in a poem feels about things.

CHECK IN 1 2 3 4

You and I

How does the poet use figurative language to help you understand her message?

Talk About It Reread the second stanza on **Literature Anthology** page 474. Discuss with your partner what "splits us each in two" means.

Cite Text Evidence What phrases help you understand the poet's message? Write text evidence and tell the message.

Text Evidence	Message

Write The poet helps me see the message _____

_____

_____

_____

Quick Tip

Think about the subjects of the poem, *you* and *I*. How does the poet connect the two?

Evaluate Information

You can evaluate the details in a poem to determine its message. How does the poet present the message? Explain whether you agree or disagree with the poem's message.

CHECK IN 1 2 3 4

My Goal **I can use text evidence to respond to poetry.**

Respond to Reading

COLLABORATE

Discuss the prompt below. Use your notes and text evidence to support your answer.

Why are connections with others so important? How do the metaphors and other figurative language in the poems help show this importance?

_____

_____

_____

_____

_____

_____

_____

_____

_____

_____

_____

_____

_____

_____

_____

Quick Tip

Use these sentence starters to talk about and cite text evidence.

• *The metaphors in the first poem . . .*

• *The figurative language in the second poem . . .*

• *These techniques show that people can connect with each other by . . .*

CHECK IN 1 2 3 4

A Time to Talk

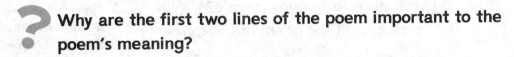 **Why are the first two lines of the poem important to the poem's meaning?**

Talk About It Reread the poem on **Literature Anthology** page 476. Discuss with your partner what the speaker is saying in the first two lines.

Cite Text Evidence What clues help you understand how the first two lines affect the rest of the poem? Write text evidence.

Text Evidence

↓

↓

↓

How It's Important

Write The first two lines affect the rest of the poem because _____

_____

CHECK IN 1 > 2 > 3 > 4 >

? **What do you learn about the speaker from this poem?**

Talk About It Reread the poem on **Literature Anthology** page 476. With a partner, talk about what choice the speaker of the poem has to make.

Cite Text Evidence What words and phrases describe what kind of person the speaker is? Write text evidence in the web.

Quick Tip

Think about the speaker's actions. What does this tell you about his or her qualities?

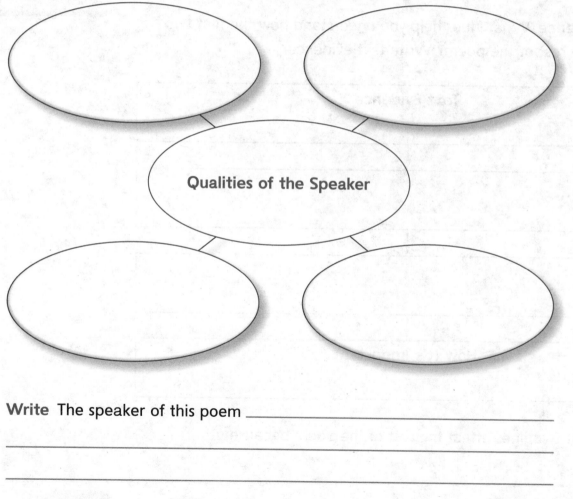

Qualities of the Speaker

Write The speaker of this poem _____

_____

_____

_____

CHECK IN 〉 1 〉 2 〉 3 〉 4 〉

Imagery

Imagery is created by the words writers choose to describe ideas, actions, places, or things. Poets use imagery to create mental images for readers to deepen their understanding. Imagery can also appeal to the senses and create a mood, or feeling, in a poem or narrative.

FIND TEXT EVIDENCE

In "A Time to Talk" on **Literature Anthology** page 476, the poet uses imagery to create a scene in which a farmer stops work to talk to a friend. Vivid words such as *thrust* show the action. The words *hoe, go,* and *stone* emphasize the long *o* sound. The word *mellow,* as used here, means "soft" and gives a sense of what the ground is like.

> I thrust my hoe in the mellow ground,
> Blade-end up and five feet tall.

Your Turn Reread lines 7–8 of the poem on page 476.

- How does the poet use imagery to help you visualize the hoe?

  _____

  _____

- What mood does the poet create in the last two lines of the poem?

  _____

  _____

Readers to Writers

Choose precise words to create imagery in your writing. For example, if you want to create a vivid picture and feeling of an approaching storm, use sensory words such as *biting* or *chilling* instead of *cold* to describe the wind. A thesaurus will help you find just the right words.

CSP_schankz/Fotosearch LBRF/age fotostock

CHECK IN 1 2 3 4

Integrate | MAKE CONNECTIONS

 How are the connections in this painting similar to the connections in the poems "You Are My Music" and "A Time to Talk"?

Quick Tip

Think about what the children are doing and how they might feel. This can help you compare this painting with the poems you read.

 Talk About It Look at the painting and read the caption. Talk with a partner about what you see in the painting.

Cite Text Evidence **Circle** the examples of connections you see in this painting. Reread the caption and **underline** evidence that helps you understand what connections to the world can teach us.

Write The connections in the painting and in the poems are similar because _____

_____

_____

_____

_____

_____

_____

_____

_____

Peter Hansen's painting "Playing Children, Enghave Square" was created in 1907-1908. It shows children playing in their neighborhood park on a sunny day.

CHECK IN 1 2 3 4

My Goal I know what our connections to the world can teach us.

Write a Poem

You read about people who interact with familiar friends and make new ones. You also read about people who try new experiences or visit new places. What have these people learned from the connections they made?

1 Look at your Build Knowledge notes in your reader's notebook.

2 Write a poem about why connecting with others from different places, cultures, and customs is meaningful.

3 Give examples from what you read to support your ideas. Use new vocabulary words.

Think about what you learned in this text set. Fill in the bars on page 169.

MY GOALS

Think about what you already know. Fill in the bars. Now let's get started!

Key

1 = I do not understand.

2 = I understand but need more practice.

3 = I understand.

4 = I understand and can teach someone.

What I Know Now

I can write a historical fiction story.

| 1 | 2 | 3 | 4 |

I can write a narrative poem.

| 1 | 2 | 3 | 4 |

Think about what you learned. Fill in the bars. The more you write, the more you'll improve.

What I Learned

I can write a historical fiction story.

1 2 3 4

I can write a narrative poem.

1 2 3 4

Expert Model

Features of Historical Fiction

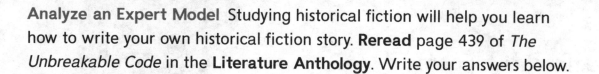

Historical fiction is based on real people, places, or events from the past. It can be told from different points of view. However, some details, such as the characters or what the characters say to each other, are made up. Historical fiction

- features plot events, including a conflict that the main character faces;

- tells events in a logical sequence;

- includes narrative techniques such as dialogue, description, and pacing.

Literature Anthology:
pages 430–443

Analyze an Expert Model Studying historical fiction will help you learn how to write your own historical fiction story. **Reread** page 439 of *The Unbreakable Code* in the **Literature Anthology**. Write your answers below.

What words and phrases does the author use to help you understand the sequence of events? _____

_____

_____

What details in the second paragraph tell you that the memory is a difficult one for Grandfather? _____

_____

_____

HomeStudio/Shutterstock

Plan: Choose Your Topic

Mapping With a partner, talk about different periods of history that interest you or a time period in history you learned about. Then think about some characters who might live during those times and what they might do. On a sheet of paper, make idea webs of different periods with characters and conflicts they might face. Consider the significant events that happened during that historical period as you map out your characters and conflicts and how those events might have affected your characters.

Writing Prompt Choose one historical period from your idea webs. Write a story about characters from that period and events that take place during that time in history. Remember that stories usually have a conflict, or problem, that needs to be resolved.

I will write about _____.

Purpose and Audience An **author's purpose** is his or her main reason for writing. What is your purpose for writing? Who will be your audience?

My purpose for writing my story is _____

_____.

The audience for my story will be _____

_____.

Plan In your writer's notebook, make a sequence of events graphic organizer to plan your writing. Fill in the first event.

Quick Tip

Authors often use signal words and phrases to help readers understand the sequence of events in a story. Use words or phrases such as *First, Next, After,* and *Finally* to help readers follow the sequence of events in your historical fiction story.

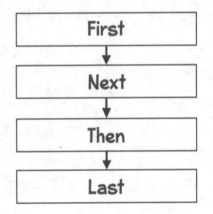

| First |
| Next |
| Then |
| Last |

CHECK IN 1 2 3 4

Plan: Characters

Develop Characters Once you have chosen your historical period and decided on some details you plan to include, you will need to think carefully about your characters. Well-developed characters can make a story come to life in the readers' minds. Ask yourself these questions:

- Have I decided on the point of view, or who is telling the story? Is my narrator a character in the story? What is my narrator's relationship to the other characters?

- Have I thought carefully about my characters' personalities?

- How might I use more descriptive language to make a character more interesting? Am I using vivid descriptive adjectives?

- What do I want my characters to do, act, or feel?

List two characters you might use in your story and describe them.

_____

_____

_____

_____

_____

Take Notes Now go back to your sequence of events graphic organizer in your writer's notebook. Fill in the second, third, and fourth event boxes.

CHECK IN 1 2 3 4

Draft

Develop Plot The plot is what happens in a story. It usually includes a setting, a conflict that the characters must solve, and a resolution. Think about how the historical setting influences the plot as you read this example from "Shipped Out."

> My name is Libby Kendall, and I am a prisoner of war. Well, not really, but some days it feels that way. Just like my dad, I've packed up my things and shipped out. Unlike my dad, however, nothing I do will ever help the Allies win World War II.

Use the paragraph above for ideas as you begin a paragraph for your story. Introduce details about the setting. Also, think about details that indicate foreshadowing, or giving clues, about the plot events that happen later as the story progresses. Authors use foreshadowing to move the plot forward.

Quick Tip

Sometimes authors of historical fiction stories tell events out of order so that the readers can understand what happened in the past. They may also use flashbacks to explain why a past event is significant to how a character responds in the future. When authors use flashbacks or tell events out of order, they use signal words to make the events clear to the readers. For example, pay attention to words and phrases such as *two weeks ago, earlier that year, later on,* and *after many days.*

Write a Draft Use your sequence of events graphic organizer to help you write a draft in your writer's notebook. Remember to include a conflict and a resolution in your draft. Remember to indent each paragraph.

Digital Tools

For information on how to use a story map, watch the "Story Map to Draft" tutorial. Go to **my.mheducation.com**.

CHECK IN 1 2 3 4

Revise

Dialogue and Pacing Strong writers use dialogue. Dialogue reveals a character's thoughts and feelings. It also shows how a character responds to certain people or events. For example, if one character says "No!" to another character and then quickly leaves, readers can infer that the first character may be in a rush to go somewhere or might be mad at the second character.

Writers also consider how much dialogue to include in a narrative. Too much dialogue might make readers speed through events in a story and miss some details. Too little dialogue may slow down events. Using just the right amount of dialogue keeps the events moving at the right speed, or pace, and advances the plot. Pacing also keeps readers interested.

Read the example below from "Shipped Out."

> My face grew hot, but my hands felt cold. "You can't just leave," I said. I stomped on the floor for emphasis and stormed off to my bedroom.

How does this line of dialogue reveal the character's thoughts? How does it develop events?

_____

_____

_____

Grammar Connections

When you write dialogue, everything characters say is in quotation marks. Use a comma to separate words such as *he said* from the quotation itself. For example: *He said, "I have soccer practice."*

When a new character begins speaking, start with a new line. Also include a comma to indicate direct address. For example: *Dad said, "Libby, talk to me."*

Revision Revise your draft, and check that you have used dialogue to develop events. Make sure that the pacing of your story makes sense.

CHECK IN 1 2 3 4

kali9/E+/Getty Images

Peer Conferences

COLLABORATE

Review a Draft Listen carefully as a partner reads his or her work aloud. Take notes about what you liked and what was difficult to follow. Begin by telling what you liked about the draft. Use these sentence starters to help you discuss your partner's draft.

I liked your description of this character because . . .

I have a question about this line of dialogue . . .

This event is unclear to me. Can you explain why . . . ?

After you finish giving each other feedback, reflect on the peer conference. What suggestion did you find to be the most helpful?

_____

_____

_____

_____

✓ Revising Checklist

☐ Does my writing fit my purpose and audience?

☐ Do the plot and my sequence of events make sense?

☐ Do I include the right amount of dialogue to fit the pacing of my story?

☐ Is there a conflict and a resolution in my story?

☐ Are my characters well-developed? Is my character's point of view consistent throughout?

Revision After you finish your peer conference, use the Revising Checklist to help you make your historical fiction story better. Remember to use the full narrative rubric on pages 224–227 to help you with your revision.

Edit and Proofread

When you **edit** and **proofread** your writing, you look for and correct mistakes in spelling, punctuation, capitalization, and grammar. Reading through a revised draft multiple times can help you make sure you're correcting any errors. Use the checklist below to edit your sentences.

Grammar Connections

As you proofread your story, make sure that you have capitalized historic events, proper names, and abbreviations such as *Mr.*, *Mrs.*, and *Dr.*

✔ Editing Checklist

☐ Do all sentences begin with a capital letter and end with a punctuation mark?

☐ Are there any run-on sentences, sentence fragments, or sentences with incorrect subject-verb agreement?

☐ Are proper nouns capitalized?

☐ Are quotation marks used correctly?

☐ Are adverbs and descriptive adjectives used correctly?

☐ Are all words spelled correctly?

List two mistakes you found as you proofread your story.

1 _____

_____

2 _____

_____

Firma V/Shutterstock

Publish, Present, and Evaluate

Publishing When you publish your writing, you create a clean final copy that is free of mistakes. As you write your final draft be sure to write legibly in cursive. Check that you are holding your pencil or pen correctly.

Presentation When you are ready to present your work, rehearse your presentation. Use the Presenting Checklist to help you.

Evaluate After you publish your writing, use the full narrative rubric on pages 224–227 to evaluate your presentation.

What did you do successfully?

_____

What needs more work?

_____

_____

_____

Turn to page 191. Fill in the bars to show what you learned.

☑ Presenting Checklist

- ☐ Stand up straight.
- ☐ Look at the audience.
- ☐ Speak slowly, clearly, and loudly.
- ☐ Answer questions thoughtfully.

My Score			
Purpose, Focus, & Organization (4 pts)	Elaboration (4 pts)	Conventions (2 pts)	Total (10 pts)

My Goal

I can write a narrative poem.

Expert Model

Features of a Narrative Poem

A narrative poem is a type of poem that tells a story. A narrative poem

- tells a story in verse form, may contain characters, setting, and plot events, and may be told using first-person point of view

- usually includes figurative language

- often contains descriptive concrete words and sensory language

Literature Anthology: pages 472–473

Analyze an Expert Model Studying other narrative poems will help you learn how to plan and write a narrative poem of your own. **Reread** "You Are My Music" on pages 472–473 in the **Literature Anthology**. Write your answers to the questions below.

What words and phrases does the poet use to help you understand the sequence of events? _____

_____

_____

Give two examples of sensory language from "You Are My Music." Why do you think the poet chose this language? _____

_____

_____

Word Wise

Poets often use sensory language in narrative poems. Sensory language appeals to the five senses. This helps readers create a mental image while they read, complete with sounds, sights, and sometimes even smells and tastes. Read aloud the first line of the fourth stanza in "You Are My Music" on page 472. Think about the mental image it creates of Aida in the florist's shop.

Plan: Choose Your Topic

COLLABORATE

Freewrite On the lines below, write about ways you have helped your community. Maybe you volunteered to clean up the classroom, raised money, or helped younger kids with their homework. Make a list.

_____

_____

Writing Prompt Choose one idea from your list. Write a narrative poem about the topic you chose. Remember to include some details about how you helped the community.

I will write about _____

Purpose and Audience Think about who will read or hear your poem. Will your purpose be to inform, persuade, or entertain them?

My purpose for writing a narrative poem is to _____

The audience will be _____

The language I will use in my poem will be _____

_____

Plan In your writer's notebook, make a details web that lists some of the details you will include in your poem. Fill in at least two details.

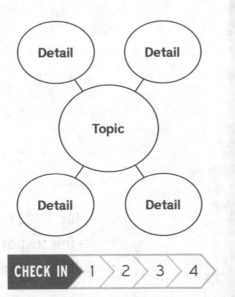

CHECK IN 1 2 3 4

Plan: Characters, Setting, and Plot

Develop a Story Narrative poetry tells a story from beginning to end. It features characters and can include dialogue. It may take place in a specific setting or time period. It includes plot events, such as conflict and resolution.

Narrative poetry is free verse. This means it may or may not rhyme. It also may or may not include meter, or a regular repeated pattern of sounds. It often includes imagery, or descriptive language.

As you plan your first draft, ask yourself these questions:

- Who is the speaker of this poem? Is the speaker a character? If so, have I used the correct form of point of view?

- What details do I need to set up this scene for my readers? What details can I add to make the conflict and resolution clear to readers?

- What do I want the dialogue between certain characters to reveal about the characters themselves?

- How can I use descriptive details to convey the overall message I want to share with my readers?

Think about the conflict in your narrative poem. How is the conflict resolved?

_____

_____

Graphic Organizer Once you've decided on all the details you will include, fill in the rest of your details web. If you need more space to write your details, use a separate sheet of paper in your writer's notebook.

Word Wise

A prepositional phrase can act as an adverb that tells how, when, or where.

For example, in the lines "Thunder is nature's clatter / that vibrates in my ears," the phrase "in my ears" is a prepositional phrase that tells where something is.

CHECK IN ▷ 1 ▷ 2 ▷ 3 ▷ 4

Draft

Figurative Language Poets often use figurative language to help readers create mental images and deepen understanding. Figurative language includes metaphor, simile, personification, imagery, alliteration, and hyperbole. Read the lines below. In the poem, a metaphor is used to compare making a change with a key in a door.

> And then I had to ask myself,
> What was I waiting for?
> The change can start with me, you see,
> That key is in my door.

Now use the lines above as a model to write lines that might be included in your narrative poem. Include an example of figurative language.

_____

_____

_____

_____

Word Wise

A simile compares two things by using the words *like* or *as*—for example, *the song was like an old friend greeting me*. A metaphor is a direct comparison that refers to one thing as another, but does not use the words *like* or *as*—for example, *the song was an old friend greeting me*.

 Write a Draft Use your details web to help you write your draft in your writer's notebook. Use figurative language in your poem. Remember that your narrative poem is telling a story and should include plot events. Check that your narrative poem has a beginning, middle, and end. It is up to you if you choose to indent certain lines in your poem.

CHECK IN 1 2 3 4

Revise

Concrete Words and Sensory Language Poets create mental images for readers by using vivid descriptive concrete words and sensory language. Concrete words name things we can know through our senses, like *red*, *hot*, and *car*. Sensory language includes words that appeal to the five senses (taste, touch, sight, smell, and sound). For example, "we ran through the soft green grass" helps the reader understand the speaker's experience more than "we ran through the grass."

Read the lines below. Then revise them so they contain more concrete words and create stronger mental images.

> When I sat down at the piano, I felt so nervous.
> But as soon as I started to play, I became calm.

_____

_____

_____

_____

 Revision Revise your draft. Check that you have used enough sensory details, figurative language, and concrete words to help your reader really understand the experience you are describing.

CHECK IN 1 2 3 4

Quick Tip

Close your eyes while a friend reads your draft to you. Do the words help you accurately visualize what is happening? What descriptive sensory language can you add to help your reader better visualize what is happening?

Peer Conferences

Review a Draft Listen carefully as a partner reads his or her work aloud. Take notes about what you liked and what was difficult to follow. Begin by telling what you liked about the draft. Ask questions or make suggestions that will make a stronger poem. Use these sentence starters.

I enjoyed your description of this character because ...

More concrete words or sensory language would help me visualize ...

I have a question about this metaphor because ...

After you finish giving each other feedback, reflect on the peer conference. What suggestion did you find to be the most helpful?

_____

_____

_____

Revision After you finish your peer conference, use the Revising Checklist to help you make your narrative poem better. Remember to use the full narrative rubric on pages 224–227 to help you with your revision.

✔ Revising Checklist

☐ Does my poem tell a story? Does it have a conflict and resolution?

☐ What details can I add to help my readers better understand the characters' feelings and actions in the poem? Is my character's point of view consistent throughout the poem?

☐ Do I use enough figurative language to help my readers fully visualize the poem?

☐ Are there places where additional concrete and sensory words would improve my poem?

Edit and Proofread

When you **edit** and **proofread** your writing, you look for and correct mistakes in spelling, punctuation, capitalization, and grammar. Reading through a revised draft multiple times can help you make sure you're catching any errors. Use the checklist below to edit your sentences.

Grammar Connections

Use *more, better,* and *worse* to compare two people, places, or things. Use *most, best,* and *worst* to compare more than two people, places, or things.

✔ Editing Checklist

☐ If you used dialogue, are quotation marks used correctly?

☐ Are all prepositional phrases used correctly?

☐ Are proper nouns capitalized?

☐ Are descriptive adjectives used correctly, including comparative and superlative forms?

☐ Are all words spelled correctly?

List two mistakes you found as you proofread your narrative poem.

1 _____

_____

2 _____

_____

Publish, Present, and Evaluate

Publishing When you publish your writing, you create a clean final copy that is free of mistakes. As you write your final draft be sure to write legibly in cursive. Check that you are holding your pencil or pen correctly and are correctly spacing words.

Presentation When you are ready to present your work, rehearse your presentation. Use the Presenting Checklist to help you.

Evaluate After you publish your writing, use the full narrative rubric on pages 224–227 to evaluate your presentation.

What did you do successfully?

_____

What needs more work?

_____

_____

_____

_____

✓ **Presenting Checklist**

☐ Look at the audience and make eye contact.

☐ Speak clearly with expression.

☐ Match your reading rate to the feelings you are describing.

☐ Use natural gestures and appropriate volume as you speak.

Turn to page 191. Fill in the bars to show what you learned.

My Score			
Purpose, Focus, & Organization (4 pts)	Elaboration (4 pts)	Conventions (2 pts)	Total (10 pts)

My Goal

I can read and understand social studies texts.

TAKE NOTES

Take notes and annotate as you read the passages "Sarah Winnemucca: Word Warrior" and "Sequoyah's Gift."

Look for the answer to the question: *What conclusions can you draw about Native Americans' contributions?*

_____

_____

_____

_____

_____

_____

_____

_____

_____

_____

_____

_____

PASSAGE 1

NARRATIVE NONFICTION

SARAH WINNEMUCCA:
WORD WARRIOR

Sarah Winnemucca is an important figure in American history. She was a Native American who fought for equality among all people. Through education and public service, she used the power of words to raise awareness for her people, the Paiute.

Born in 1844, Winnemucca learned English when she was thirteen years old. For most of her childhood, she lived on her homelands in Paiute territory, in what is now western Nevada. In the 1860s, the US government forced the Native Americans to live on reservations.

Because Winnemucca knew English, she was called on to serve as an interpreter between US government agents and the Paiute reservation. One government agent didn't respect the tribal leaders. He didn't honor many agreements made with the previous agent. In 1876, he fired Winnemucca when she sent the concerns of the Paiute to Washington, D.C. Then, in 1879, the Paiute were forced to move hundreds of miles away to Washington state. The Paiute suffered from hunger and poverty.

Winnemucca was so angry that she started speaking out against the mistreatment of her people and other Native Americans on reservations. In her public lectures, Winnemucca asked Americans to live up to their political ideals about justice for all. She explained that many Native American women and children were injured in attacks. She helped people see the bias in newspaper headlines. She asked them to respect her identity and humanity as a Native American.

Magenta10/Shutterstock

Winnemucca made sure that Paiute culture wasn't forgotten. She started a school for Paiute children. Her book *Life Among the Paiutes* was published in 1883. In her book, she stressed that Native Americans have the right to live their lives as they choose to. Her book was significant for two reasons. It was the first book written by a Native American woman, and it was also the first to describe Paiute culture.

In 1884, Congress passed a bill to set aside land for the Paiute. Though the government did not keep its promise, Winnemucca's efforts are not forgotten. She died in 1891, but her book is still read and used in schools. Today, her statue is one of two representing Nevada in the US Capitol.

Sarah Winnemucca holds a shellflower in her right hand and a book in her left. Her given name, Thocmetony, means "shellflower."

Magenta10/Shutterstock; Architect of the Capitol

SARAH WINNEMUCCA

1844 – 1891

NEVADA
DEFENDER OF HUMAN RIGHTS
EDUCATOR
AUTHOR OF FIRST BOOK BY A NATIVE WOMAN

TAKE NOTES

PASSAGE 2 — EXPOSITORY TEXT

Sequoyah's Gift

Legend says the Cherokee people once had a way to write their language, but it was lost long ago. But when Sequoyah was young, there was no way to write in Cherokee. He became determined to invent one.

Sequoyah was born to a Cherokee mother in Tennessee around 1775. After moving to Georgia, he fought in the US Army during the Creek War in 1813–1814. Before the war, Sequoyah was already experimenting with pictographs, or picture symbols. He was trying to find a way to develop his own Cherokee writing system. The war made him realize he had to keep trying. Only troops who read English could read orders and write letters.

In 1821, Sequoyah gave the Cherokee chiefs a finished syllabary, or a type of alphabet that uses symbols for syllables. He's the only person in history to invent an entire alphabet. In just a few years, many Cherokee were reading and writing. In 1828, the Cherokee printed the first Native American newspaper in the nation.

Sequoyah's gift of his syllabary changed his people's lives. He died in 1843, but his memory lives on. The tall sequoia tree of the US West and Sequoia National Park in California are named for Sequoyah.

Sequoyah and his syllabary

North Wind Picture Archives/Alamy Stock Photo

COMPARE THE PASSAGES

Review your notes from "Sarah Winnemucca: Word Warrior" and "Sequoyah's Gift." Then use your notes to complete the chart below.

Point to Compare	Passage 1	Passage 2
Main Life Events		
What the Person Is Remembered For		
How the Person Is Honored		
Your Opinion of Her or His Accomplishments		
Supporting Detail for Your Opinion		

Synthesize Information

Think about what you learned in these two texts. How do the topics of these texts help you understand the contributions of Native Americans in *The Unbreakable Code* and "Allies in Action"? Write your ideas in your reader's notebook.

CHECK IN 1 2 3 4

RESEARCH HISTORICAL INFORMATION

Figures who stand out in history are often the subjects of biographies. Biographical texts include historical details, such as how people lived or worked at the time. Biographies cover many subjects, even if the focus is on certain people.

With a partner, discuss the ways the two texts about Sarah Winnemucca and Sequoyah also tell readers about US history.

Then, complete the blanks below. Choose either Sarah Winnemucca or Sequoyah. Use the passages as a starting point. Refer to reliable print and digital resources to find more information about the time period when that person lived. Remember to write down the sources you used. You may use your reader's notebook.

Sarah Winnemucca/Sequoyah was born in _____

and died in _____. Winnemucca/Sequoyah

worked as a _____. At that time, this meant

_____. During those years, the United States went

through many changes and events, including _____.
The way this affected Winnemucca/Sequoyah was

_____. Winnemucca/Sequoyah faced personal

challenges, such as _____. Winnemucca/Sequoyah

changed history by _____.

WRITE ABOUT A MEMORY

Sarah Winnemucca's book is called *Life Among the Paiutes: Their Wrongs and Claims*. It is a history of her people and also a memoir. A memoir is a collection of memories from a person's life.

Think about your own life. Write about one memory that you would include in a memoir. Your memory can be from any time in your life. As you write about your memory, ask yourself these questions:

- Do I give enough details about when and where this memory took place?

- Do my descriptions give readers mental images of my memory?

- Do the events in my memory make logical sense? Did I use enough transitional words to connect events together?

- Have I explained how I feel about this memory or why this memory is important to me?

When writing about your memory, describe ideas in detail. You can write about friends, family members, school, food, music, sports, and more. To give readers a more vivid mental image, include sensory language. How do things look, sound, smell, taste, or feel?

Use your reader's notebook if you need more space than the lines below. After you have completed your memory, you will present it to the class.

_____

_____

_____

_____

My Goal I can read and understand science texts.

TAKE NOTES

Take notes and annotate as you read the passages "Wonders of the Water Cycle" and "An Ocean of Adaptations."

Look for the answer to the question: *What helps living things survive when their environment changes?*

_____

_____

_____

_____

_____

_____

_____

_____

_____

_____

_____

PASSAGE 1   EXPOSITORY TEXT

WONDERS of the WATER CYCLE

Water is a wonder. It can be a solid, a liquid, or a gas. Through natural processes, water can take different forms while moving on, above, or even below the ground.

At any given time, most of the world's water is in storage, with the ocean holding nearly 97 percent. However, at the same time, the world's water is on the move. This movement is called the water cycle. For example, liquid water becomes water vapor in a process called evaporation. Water is made of parts called molecules. If heat breaks the bonds that hold the molecules together, water can rise as a gas. The water vapor cools into water droplets and ice crystals as it rises and forms clouds. This process is called condensation. The water in a cloud can fall back to Earth as precipitation. It can fall as rain, which is liquid, or appear more solid and fall as snow or hail.

The Water Cycle

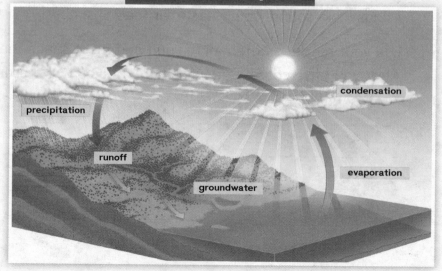

Some precipitation falls into bodies of water, and some falls on the ground, becoming groundwater. Other precipitation becomes runoff, which travels across land in streams, heading back to the ocean. Meanwhile, plants, animals, and humans consume a portion of the fresh water produced by these processes. The water cycle is the way water passes to and from the air, land, and bodies of water.

Living things on land need to consume fresh water, or low-salt water, to live. Salts are found throughout the ocean, making ocean water undrinkable. Today, humans cannot use 99 percent of Earth's water because it is undrinkable. But scientists are hoping to change that percentage. They are finding new ways to increase drinkable water options while protecting the water cycle.

EXPOSITORY TEXT

An Ocean of Adaptations

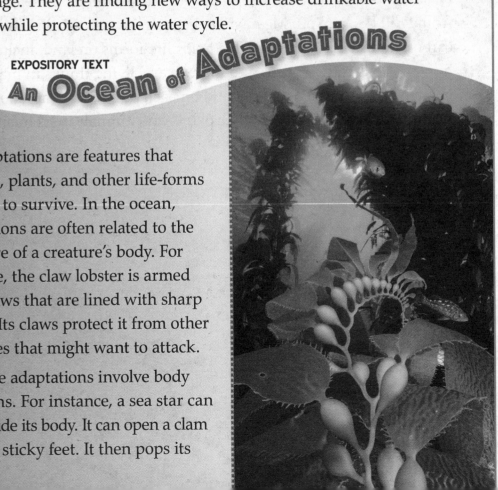

Adaptations are features that animals, plants, and other life-forms develop to survive. In the ocean, adaptations are often related to the structure of a creature's body. For example, the claw lobster is armed with claws that are lined with sharp spines. Its claws protect it from other creatures that might want to attack.

Some adaptations involve body functions. For instance, a sea star can eat outside its body. It can open a clam with its sticky feet. It then pops its

Douglas Klug/Getty Images

_____

_____

_____

_____

_____

_____

_____

_____

_____

_____

_____

_____

_____

_____

_____

_____

_____

_____

_____

_____

_____

_____

_____

stomach out, slips its tummy into the opened shell, and turns its prey into mush so it can digest it. A sea star's body chemicals make this possible.

Adaptations also have to do with behaviors. Many smaller creatures, such as herring, have learned to travel in large groups. This confuses predators and makes it difficult for them to catch individual fish.

Some living things have both body and behavioral adaptations. Kelp is a kind of algae. It has a balloon-like adaptation that pulls it upright in water. This helps it anchor to rocks on the ocean floor. It has learned to gather with other kelp. A grouping of kelp looks like a forest. Sea otters have learned to rest in these kelp forests, where they prey on other creatures that want to eat the kelp. Without sea otters, these creatures would kill the kelp off. Meanwhile, kelp cleans a wondrous amount of carbon dioxide from the air. This helps life-forms on land, including humans, to breathe. In this and many ways, living things in many habitats are connected and depend on each other. An adaptation of one plant or animal can impact other plants and animals in its habitat.

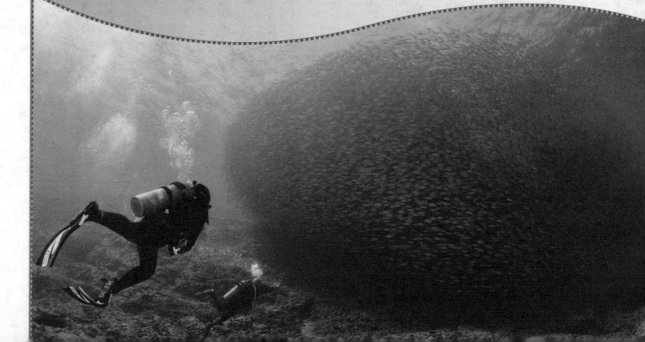

Hudson Fleece/Alamy Stock Photo

COMPARE THE PASSAGES

Review your notes from "Wonders of the Water Cycle" and "An Ocean of Adaptations." Create a Venn diagram like the one below. Use your notes and the diagram to record how information in these texts is alike and different.

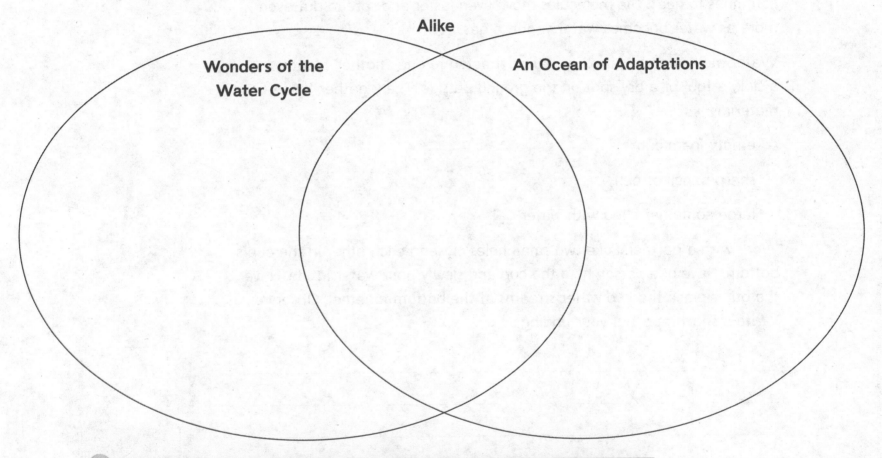

Alike

Wonders of the Water Cycle

An Ocean of Adaptations

Synthesize Information

Think about what you learned in these two texts. How does this information help you understand what living things need to survive? Write your ideas in your reader's notebook.

CHECK IN 1 2 3 4

OBSERVE WATER MOLECULES IN ACTION

When water gets colder, its molecules slow down and form rigid bonds, creating solid ice. When ice warms and melts, the molecules move faster and spread out, sliding around each other as liquid water. As water continues to heat, the molecules move even faster and spread out even more as water becomes water vapor, a gas.

Water molecules are also naturally attracted to one another. Identify a sink, a tub, or a dry spot on the ground outside. Then, gather these materials:

*   empty foam cup

*   sharp pencil or pen

*   large container filled with water

Work with a partner. Poke two small holes close to each other in the cup's bottom. Have one person hold the cup and slowly pour water inside. Have the other pinch the two water streams at the bottom together. Observe. Write a short report of your findings.

_____

_____

_____

_____

_____

_____

Reflect on Your Learning

Talk About It Reflect on what you learned in this unit. Then talk with a partner about how you did.

I am really proud of how I can _____

_____

_____

_____

Something I need to work more on is _____

_____

_____

_____

_____

My Goal Congratulations on all that you've accomplished this year! What are your goals for next year? In your reader's notebook, write about what you can do to get there.

Share a goal you have with a partner.

Expository Writing Rubric

Score	Purpose, Focus, and Organization (4-point Rubric)	Evidence and Elaboration (4-point Rubric)	Conventions of Standard English (2-point Rubric begins at score point 2)
4	• stays focused on the purpose, audience, and task • clearly presents and fully develops the central idea about a topic • uses transitional strategies, such as words and phrases, to connect ideas • uses a logical text structure to organize information • begins with a strong introduction and ends with a strong conclusion	• effectively supports the central idea with convincing facts and details • has strong examples of relevant evidence, or supporting details, from multiple sources • uses elaborative techniques, such as facts, examples, definitions, and quotations from sources • expresses interesting ideas clearly using precise language • uses appropriate academic and domain-specific language • uses different sentence structures	

Score	Purpose, Focus, and Organization (4-point Rubric)	Evidence and Elaboration (4-point Rubric)	Conventions of Standard English (2-point Rubric begins at score point 2)
3	• generally stays focused on the purpose, audience, and task • presents and develops the central idea about a topic in a mostly clear and complete way, although there may be some unimportant details • uses some transitional strategies, such as words and phrases, to connect ideas • uses a mostly logical text structure to organize information • begins with an acceptable introduction and ends with a sufficient conclusion	• mostly supports the central idea with some convincing facts and details • has some examples of mostly relevant evidence, or supporting details, from multiple sources • uses some elaborative techniques, such as facts, examples, definitions, and quotations from sources • generally expresses interesting ideas using both precise and general language • mostly uses appropriate academic and domain-specific language • mostly uses different sentence structures	

Expository Writing Rubric

Score	Purpose, Focus, and Organization (4-point Rubric)	Evidence and Elaboration (4-point Rubric)	Conventions of Standard English (2-point Rubric)
2	• stays somewhat focused on the purpose, audience, and task, but may include unimportant details • does not clearly present or develop a central idea • uses few transitional strategies to connect ideas • may not follow a logical text structure to organize information • may begin with an inadequate introduction or end with an unsatisfactory conclusion	• shows some support of the central idea with few convincing facts and details • has weak and inappropriate examples of evidence or does not include enough sources • may not use elaborative techniques effectively • expresses some interesting ideas, but ideas are simple and vague • uses limited academic and domain-specific language • may use only simple sentence structures	• has a sufficient command of grammar and usage • has a sufficient command of capitalization, punctuation, spelling, and sentence formation • has slight errors in grammar and usage that do not affect meaning

Score	Purpose, Focus, and Organization (4-point Rubric)	Evidence and Elaboration (4-point Rubric)	Conventions of Standard English (2-point Rubric)
1	• is not aware of the purpose, audience, and task • does not have a central idea • uses few or no transitional strategies to connect ideas • does not follow a logical text structure to organize information • does not include an introduction nor a conclusion	• supports the central idea with few facts and details or does not support the central idea at all • has few or no examples of evidence or does not include enough sources • does not use elaborative techniques • has confusing or unclear ideas or does not express any interesting ideas • does not demonstrate a grasp of academic and domain-specific language • consists only of simple sentence structures	• has an incomplete command of grammar and usage • has an incomplete command of capitalization, punctuation, spelling, and sentence formation • has some errors in grammar and usage that may affect meaning
0			• does not have a command of grammar and usage • does not have a command of capitalization, punctuation, spelling, and sentence formation • has too many serious errors in grammar and usage that frequently disrupt meaning

Narrative Writing Rubric

Score	Purpose, Focus, and Organization (4-point Rubric)	Elaboration (4-point Rubric)	Conventions of Standard English (2-point Rubric begins at score point 2)
4	• stays focused on the purpose, audience, and task • presents a fictional or personal narrative in which the story is clearly told from a first-, second-, or third-person point of view • develops an imagined or real narrative, setting, and/or characters • uses transitional strategies, such as words and phrases, to connect ideas and events • presents a logical sequence of events that tells a story with a clear beginning, middle, and end	• uses dialogue and description effectively • uses different narrative techniques that advance the story, illustrate the experience, or keep readers interested • uses sensory, concrete, and figurative language successfully • uses different sentence structures	

Score	Purpose, Focus, and Organization (4-point Rubric)	Elaboration (4-point Rubric)	Conventions of Standard English (2-point Rubric begins at score point 2)
3	• generally stays focused on the purpose, audience, and task • presents a fictional or personal narrative in which the story is mostly clearly told from a first-, second-, or third-person point of view • develops a satisfactory imagined or real narrative, setting, and/or characters • uses some transitional strategies, such as words and phrases, to connect ideas and events • presents a mostly logical sequence of events that tells a story with an acceptable beginning, middle, and end	• uses some dialogue and description • generally uses different narrative techniques that advance the story, illustrate the experience, or keep readers interested • uses sensory, concrete, and figurative language mostly successfully • uses some different sentence structures	

Narrative Writing Rubric

Score	Purpose, Focus, and Organization (4-point Rubric)	Elaboration (4-point Rubric)	Conventions of Standard English (2-point Rubric)
2	• stays somewhat focused on the purpose, audience, and task • presents a fictional or personal narrative in which the story is not clearly told from a first-, second-, or third-person point of view • develops an unclear or incomplete narrative, setting, and/or characters • uses few transitional strategies, such as words and phrases, to connect ideas and events • may present a sequence of events that does not tell a complete story or includes an inadequate beginning and ending	• uses some dialogue and description, but some details are unclear • uses weak or ineffective narrative techniques • may use some sensory, concrete, and figurative language, but examples may be limited • may use only simple sentence structures	• has a sufficient command of grammar and usage • has a sufficient command of capitalization, punctuation, spelling, and sentence formation • has a few errors in grammar and usage that do not affect meaning

Score	Purpose, Focus, and Organization (4-point Rubric)	Elaboration (4-point Rubric)	Conventions of Standard English (2-point Rubric)
1	• is not aware of the purpose, audience, and task • does not present a fictional or personal narrative, and there is no narrator's point of view • does not develop a narrative, setting, and/or characters • uses few or no transitional strategies, such as words and phrases, to connect ideas and events • tells a confusing story with no sequence of events	• uses little or no dialogue or descriptiion • uses few or no narrative techniques • has confusing, unclear, or no examples of sensory, concrete, and figurative language • includes only simple sentence structures	• has an incomplete command of grammar and usage • has an incomplete command of capitalization, punctuation, spelling, and sentence formation • has some errors in grammar and usage that may affect meaning
0			• does not have a command of grammar and usage • does not have a command of capitalization, punctuation, spelling, and sentence formation • has too many serious errors in grammar and usage that frequently disrupt meaning